Oklahoma Joe's™ Frequent Fryers
Frying & Boiling Cookbook

Oklahoma Joe's™

Frequent Fryers
Frying & Boiling Cookbook

Table of Contents

Introduction

The deep-fried turkey craze has swept the country, moving out of the Cajun bayous and into the mainstream. It's such a dramatic, fun and delicious way to cook a holiday bird, that everyone wants to get involved. And the fact that the turkey gets done in a fraction of the usual time has certainly fueled the trend.

The good news is that you can do a whole lot more than turkey. Great new equipment makes this outdoor style of cooking so simple, you'll want to do it year-round. Now you can whip up a big batch of succulent jelly doughnuts, a mess of crisp catfish and hush puppies, or a classic New England lobster boil without worrying about lingering odors, spilled oil or an overheated house!

As the popularity of French fries attests, our love of deep-fried foods is greater than that of any other nation in the world. But food cooked in oil is really an ancient tradition, and this book includes a selection of recipes old and new for fried delights that hail from both close-to-home and around the world; there are easy appetizers like Deep-Fried Spring Rolls, mouth-watering entrees like Oklahoma Joe's™ Sizzlin' Steaks and fabulous sweets like Fried Ice Cream—not to mention yummy vegetable fritters and savory breads. And of course, there's a complete how-to for deep-fried turkey, as delicious for a Fourth of July bash as it is on Thanksgiving day.

winter

spring

summer

fall

You can use the very same equipment to simmer a big pot of Beer-Cooked Sausage BBQ for sandwiches or steamed Mussels Meuniere, so we've included delicious recipes for crowd-pleasing boiled and steamed feasts, too.

You can deep-fry year-round: Each recipe has a handy icon at the top of the page, with the best seasons to make that dish marked in a darker shade (see inset). We've also included the best techniques for deep-frying and boiling, what kind of equipment and accessories you'll need, the best types of oil to choose and great ideas for adding exciting flavor to your dishes with special marinades, rubs and sauces.

So whether it's for tried-and-true classics like Chicken Fried Steak or exotic Indonesian Fried Bananas with Ice Cream, invite your friends and start cooking!

Breads

Biscuits in Honey Glaze

8 servings

Enjoy these as dessert or with a main course, such as ham or Breaded Pork Chops (p. 66), if you have a sweet tooth.

½ cup honey
½ stick butter
1 package frozen biscuits
  or rolls, defrosted
  Vegetable oil for deep frying

In a small saucepan, heat together the honey and butter until warm.

Make a hole in the middle of each biscuit so that it resembles a donut.

Preheat oil in a deep-fryer to 365° F.

Fry the biscuits in batches until golden all over, (about 4 minutes per batch). Remove the biscuits with a skimmer or slotted spoon, and transfer them to a tray lined with paper towels for draining.

Dip the biscuits in the melted honey butter and serve warm.

Remember never to fill your fryer more than half-full with oil.

Hush Puppies

6 servings

Hush Puppies are traditionally served with deep-fried fish, and especially as a snack on fishing trips. As a universal favorite, however, they taste good any time.

2 cups cornmeal
2 teaspoons baking powder
1 teaspoon Oklahoma Joe's™ Original BBQ seasoning
½ teaspoon salt
1 medium onion, minced
2 eggs, beaten
1 cup milk
Vegetable oil for deep frying

Preheat the oil in a deep-fryer to 365° F.

In a bowl, toss together the cornmeal, baking powder, Oklahoma Joe's™ seasoning and salt.

Add the onion, eggs and milk, and stir into a thick batter.

Carefully drop by rounded teaspoons into the hot oil. Do not crowd the pot; they will cook fast. As soon as they brown, transfer the hush puppies to a layer of paper towels to drain, and serve hot.

Remember never to fill your fryer more than half-full with oil.

Sopaipillas (New Mexican Puffed Breads)

Makes 1 dozen

These "sofa pillows" are quick to make and very versatile. They appear throughout the Southwest, served most often as a sidedish with honey butter. You can also split them open and stuff them with a meat or bean filling or roll them in cinnamon sugar for dessert.

The Honey Butter
1 stick (½ cup) butter, softened
¼ cup honey

PREPARE THE HONEY BUTTER

In a small bowl, combine butter and honey. With a whisk or electric mixer, beat together thoroughly.

Cover tightly and refrigerate, bringing to room temperature before serving.

PREPARE THE SOPAIPILLAS

Into a medium bowl, sift flour, salt and baking powder. Stir in oil. Add water and milk and stir together to form a sticky dough.

Turn the dough out onto a floured work surface and knead until no longer sticky (about 1 minute), adding a bit more flour if needed. Cover the dough with plastic wrap and set aside for 15 minutes.

Divide the dough in thirds, and shape each piece into a ball. Cover again and set aside for 20 more minutes.

Tips:

If you don't want to serve the sopaipillas right away, let them cool and put them in a plastic bag. Remove and reheat them in a 350° F. oven within a few hours. Or wrap them well and store them in the freezer for up to 2 months, and reheat them just before serving.

The Sopaipillas
  2 cups all-purpose flour
  1 teaspoon salt
  1 teaspoon baking powder
  2 teaspoons vegetable oil
  ½ cup lukewarm water
  ¼ cup milk
    Vegetable oil for deep frying

Preheat the oil in a deep-fryer to 375° F.

On a lightly floured surface, roll each ball into a ⅛-inch-thick circle, about 8 inches in diameter. Cut each circle into quarters.

About four at a time, add the sopaipillas to the oil and cook, turning occasionally, until puffed and golden on both sides (about 2 minutes). Remove with tongs and drain briefly on paper towels.

Serve immediately with honey butter.

Remember never to fill your fryer more than half-full with oil.

※ ❀ ○ ❧

Great Plains Fry-Bread

Makes 6 loaves

It's fun to make this dough from scratch, by hand or with a heavy-duty electric mixer. Ready-made dough from a supermarket or even a pizza store is usually available, too, and is an acceptable substitute.

5 cups all-purpose flour
1 package fast-acting yeast
1 teaspoon sugar
1 teaspoon baking powder
1 teaspoon salt
2 cups warm water
　Vegetable oil for deep frying

In a large bowl, combine 3 cups of the flour with the yeast, sugar, baking powder and salt.

Add the water and beat well by hand with a wooden spoon for about 5 minutes or with an electric mixer set at medium speed for about 2 minutes.

Gradually beat in enough of the remaining flour to create a soft but not sticky dough.

Turn the dough out onto a lightly floured surface, and knead it with your knuckles for 5 minutes. (With a mixer, mix on low speed for 5 minutes.) Place the dough in a large, oiled bowl, turning the dough to evenly coat it with oil. Cover the bowl with plastic wrap and set in a warm spot to rise until doubled in size (about 1 hour).

Punch down the dough, divide it into 6 pieces and shape it into balls. Flatten the balls into round discs and score a long slit across the center of each one with a sharp knife.

Arrange a tray of paper towels
for draining the cooked
loaves.

Preheat the oil in a
deep-fryer to 365° F.

Carefully lower the loaves,
1 at a time, and cook in the hot oil, turning once,
until browned (about 5 minutes).

Transfer with a skimmer to the paper towels, and
then to a baking tray in a low-temperature oven to
keep warm while you fry the remaining loaves.

Eat while fresh and still warm.

Remember never to fill your fryer more than half-full with oil.

Stuffed Spiced Poori

Makes 15 breads

Poori, very popular in Northern India and Pakistan, is a fried, unleavened bread usually made with whole wheat flour. In this stuffed version, all-purpose flour is used to lighten the dough.

The Stuffing
1 tablespoon vegetable oil
1 small onion, minced
1 1-inch piece ginger, minced
2 teaspoons ground cumin
1 cup frozen peas, thawed
1½ tablespoons all-purpose flour

PREPARE THE STUFFING

Warm the oil in a skillet, add the onion and ginger and fry until soft. Stir in cumin and cook for 30 seconds.

Transfer to a food processor and add peas. Pulse until very finely chopped. Pulse in 2 tablespoons flour. Set aside.

PREPARE THE CHUTNEY

Put mint, scallions, water, lime juice and sugar into a blender or food processor. Pulse until very finely chopped. If too thick, add a tablespoon of water. Season to taste with salt and pepper.

Preheat the oil in a deep-fryer to 375° F.

PREPARE THE DOUGH

Stir together 2 cups flour and salt. Add the oil and rub the dough between your fingertips until it feels

Tips:

When buying ginger, choose a piece that is hard and heavy, those that are light and/or wrinkled have begun to age and dry. Fresh, moist ginger will keep about a week on the counter if kept away from sun and heat. To extend its life, store ginger wrapped in a paper towel inside a plastic bag in the crisper drawer of your refrigerator.

The Chutney
  1 cup fresh mint leaves,
     lightly packed
  2 scallions, chopped coarsely
  4 tablespoons water
  2 tablespoons lime juice
  1½ teaspoons sugar
     Salt and freshly ground black
     pepper to taste

The Dough
  2 cups all-purpose flour
  ½ teaspoon salt
  2 tablespoons vegetable oil
  ½ cup water

     Vegetable oil for deep frying

like coarse crumbs. Gradually add the water and blend to form a stiff dough. Knead until smooth (about 5 minutes).

Divide into 15 pieces and roll each piece into a ball. Flatten each ball, and set a spoonful of the stuffing in the center. Encase the stuffing in the dough, pinching dough edges to seal. On a floured surface, roll out the newly formed balls of dough to make 5-inch disks.

Fry the breads in small batches, carefully immersing them in the hot oil with a long metal spoon. When puffed, turn the bread over to cook the second side. Fry for 30 seconds and remove with tongs to drain on paper towels. Serve warm.

Remember never to fill your fryer more than half-full with oil.

Ricotta Puffs

6 servings

Try serving these delicious puffs for dessert alongside orange slices—yum!

12 ounces ricotta cheese
3 eggs, lightly beaten
½ cup all-purpose flour
2 tablespoons melted butter
Finely grated zest of 1 orange
Pinch of salt
Juice of 1 orange
½ cup honey
Vegetable oil for deep frying

In a medium bowl, stir the eggs into the ricotta using a fork. Gradually stir in the flour, then add the butter, orange zest and a pinch of salt. Refrigerate batter until cold (1 to 2 hours).

In a small saucepan, boil the orange juice down to about 2 tablespoons. Stir in the honey and set aside.

Preheat the oil in a deep-fryer to 365° F. Working in batches, drop tablespoons of the batter into the hot oil and fry, turning once, until golden (1 to 2 minutes). Drain well on paper towels.

Drizzle with the warm honey mixture and serve hot.

Remember never to fill your fryer more than half-full with oil.

Appetizers

Lip-Smackin' Fried Pickles

48 pieces, about 12 servings

Serve these with beer or cocktails. Remember to pat the pickles as dry as possible before coating with batter. This will help the batter to adhere to the pickle sections and minimize splattering on contact with the hot oil.

12 whole dill pickles (1-quart jar)
1 cup all-purpose flour
½ cup cornstarch
2 teaspoons Oklahoma Joe's™ Sweet & Spicy seasoning
1 egg
1 cup beer (or water)
Vegetable oil for deep frying

Cut the pickles lengthwise into quarters and spread them in a single layer between sheets of paper towels.

In a large bowl, whisk together the flour, cornstarch and seasoning. Add the egg and beer (or water) and whisk to combine. Let the batter rest for 30 minutes. If desired, it may be poured into a jar, covered and refrigerated overnight. (If you do, stir it just before coating the pickles.)

Set a wire rack on a shallow pan for draining. Preheat the oil in a deep-fryer to 365° F.

Working in batches, add about 8 of the pickle sections to the bowl of batter. Using tongs, carefully drop the batter-coated pickles into the hot oil and fry until crisp and golden (about 4 minutes per batch).

Use a skimmer or slotted spoon to transfer the pickles to the rack. Repeat with the remaining ingredients. Serve warm, or at room temperature.

Remember never to fill your fryer more than half-full with oil.

Fried Gruyère with a Crispy Crust

8 servings

Fried mozzarella sticks are only the beginning of the possibilities when it comes to frying cheese—any firm, sharp variety will work. In this recipe, the tartness of the caper mayonnaise complements the rich Gruyère perfectly.

The Cheese
- 1½ pounds Gruyère cheese, cut into 8 ½-inch-thick triangles
- All-purpose flour, as needed
- 3 large eggs, beaten with 2 tablespoons water
- Fine, dry breadcrumbs, as needed
- Olive oil, for frying (or a mixture of olive oil and vegetable oil)

The Caper Mayonnaise
- 1 cup mayonnaise
- 2 tablespoons lemon juice
- ¼ cup capers

Coat each cheese slice with flour, patting off excess. Dip slices in egg, covering completely and letting the excess drip off. Coat thoroughly with breadcrumbs, and press crumbs onto cheese. Dip slices back in egg and again in crumbs. Press firmly. Cover and refrigerate at least 1 hour and up to 2 days—the breading will adhere to the cheese better when chilled.

Meanwhile, make sauce by whisking together mayonnaise, lemon juice and capers. The mayonnaise will mellow, and you will have only the frying to do just before serving.

Preheat the oil in a deep-fryer to 350° F.

Fry cheese in batches of 3 or 4 slices until brown and crisp. Using fryer basket, drain and transfer to paper towels. Serve hot with the caper mayonnaise.

Remember never to fill your fryer more than half-full with oil.

Deep-Fried Squash Blossoms

4 servings

A wonderful summertime dish, squash blossoms are available at farmers' markets or in your own garden; gently snip off the flower of a summer squash vine when the bloom is a vibrant orange and fully open. Fresh ricotta and mozzarella really make a difference in the flavor of this dish. If you can't find them at your specialty foods market, regular cheeses will do.

1	cup fresh, whole-milk Ricotta
¾	cup flour
1½	teaspoon salt
	Freshly ground black pepper
⅔	cup milk
1	tablespoon finely chopped fresh herbs such as parsley, thyme, lavender or rosemary
2	ounces fresh, whole-milk mozzarella
10	squash blossoms
	Vegetable shortening for deep frying
2	lemons, cut in wedges

Place ricotta in cheesecloth and tie in a sac with kitchen twine. Tie bundle onto a wooden spoon and place over a bowl to drain. The bottom of the cheesecloth should be hanging at least 1 inch from the bottom of the bowl. Let the cheese drain in the refrigerator overnight.

PREPARE THE BATTER

Whisk together flour, ½ teaspoon of the salt, a pinch of black pepper and milk in a small bowl. Cover with plastic wrap and refrigerate for at least 1 hour.

Remove ricotta from cheesecloth, discarding any liquid left in the bowl.

PREPARE THE STUFFING

Combine ricotta, herbs, mozzarella, 1 teaspoon salt and a dash of ground pepper in a small bowl. Gently spoon about 1½ tablespoons of the ricotta mixture into each blossom, taking care not to tear the blossom's petals. Gently squeeze the top of the blossom shut with your fingers by pressing the petals together.

Preheat the shortening in a deep-fryer to 375° F.

Lightly coat each blossom in batter, scraping off excess batter on the edge of the bowl. Fry the blossoms 5 at a time until lightly golden (about 2 minutes on each side). Remove to a paper-towel–lined sheet pan to drain. Serve with lemon wedges.

Remember never to fill your fryer more than half-full with oil.

Ravioli Bites

8 to 10 servings

Ravioli is best when the pasta is home-made; however, it is possible to buy acceptable ready-made fresh or frozen ravioli that will work well in a deep-fryer. Make sure to slowly thaw the frozen ones and pat them dry before cooking.

2 pounds fresh ravioli (or frozen and defrosted
¼ cup flour
Salt
Pepper
2 tablespoons chopped flat-leaf parsley
1 16-ounce can tomato sauce, heated or room temperature
Vegetable oil for deep frying

Preheat the oil in a deep-fryer to 365° F.

Spread paper towels on a large tray for draining the cooked ravioli.

Spread the ravioli on plates and pat dry, if defrosted. Dust the ravioli lightly with the flour, brushing off the excess.

Add about 10 ravioli to the hot oil and fry until golden and crisp (3 to 5 minutes). Repeat with more batches of ravioli. Serve warm, sprinkled with salt and pepper; sprinkle parsley around the edge of the plate and pass the tomato sauce for dipping.

Remember never to fill your fryer more than half-full with oil.

Fried Green Tomatoes

4 servings

Catapulted to national fame by the 1991 movie of the same name, fried green tomatoes are simply under-ripe tomatoes that are fried. This is a great way to cook these staple items when you get a hankering for them early and just can't wait!

1 egg
1 tablespoon milk
½ teaspoon salt
¼ teaspoons freshly ground black pepper
½ cup sifted all-purpose flour
½ cup plus 2 tablespoons yellow cornmeal
2 pounds green tomatoes, cut into ½-inch-thick slices Vegetable shortening for deep-frying

In a small bowl, lightly beat together the egg and the milk and set aside. In a medium bowl combine the salt, pepper, flour and cornmeal.

Preheat the shortening in a deep-fryer to 350° F.

Coat the slices in egg, removing excess liquid, then coat in cornmeal mixture, tapping to remove excess. Place on a sheet pan.

Fry the tomatoes, in a single layer, for 2 minutes per side. Remove to a paper-towel–lined tray. Serve hot.

Remember never to fill your fryer more than half-full with oil.

Tex-Mex Potato Skins

6 Servings

The variety of salsas to go with potato skins is nearly limitless, depending on what is available according to the season and the climate.

Feel free to change the red onion to scallions, the jalapenos to any other chile, to leave out the cilantro if it is not to your taste, or to add a bit of fresh oregano.

The Potato Skins
  6 baking potatoes
    Salt, to taste

The Salsa
  ½ small red onion
    Juice of 1 lime
  2 large, ripe tomatoes
  3 tablespoons chopped fresh
    cilantro
  1 to 2 jalapeños, depending
    on hotness
    Salt, to taste

Bake potatoes until soft in the center; let them cool completely.

PREPARE THE SALSA

Dice the onion, then rinse and drain it. Stir in lime juice. Cut tomatoes in half crosswise and pull out the seeds. Dice the tomatoes and add to onion. Stir in cilantro and jalapeños. Season to taste with salt and set aside until needed.

Preheat the oil in a deep-fryer to 375° F.

Cut potatoes into quarters lengthwise, then scoop out their center flesh, leaving about ¼ inch inside the skin.

Arrange a tray of paper towels for draining the cooked potato skins.

Fry the skins in a fryer basket in small batches

Vegetable oil for deep frying
Grated Monterey Jack cheese, with or without peppers

until crisp and brown (about 5 minutes). Using the fryer basket, drain them and transfer them to the paper-towel–lined tray.

Sprinkle with salt and cheese while still hot, and serve immediately with salsa, for dipping.

Remember never to fill your fryer more than half-full with oil.

Wonton Nibbles

About 8 to 12 servings

Serve these as a tasty alternative to pretzels and potato chips at your next party. You can make them ahead of time and warm them on a tray in a hot oven for a couple of minutes before serving. Wonton wrappers are available fresh or frozen in many supermarkets.

1 package wonton wrappers, 12 ounces to 1 pound, defrosted if frozen
Vegetable oil for deep frying
Hot paprika or chili powder
Salt

Cut the wrappers into ½-inch strips. Separate the strips and spread them out to air dry for about half an hour. It's fine if they have some twists and curves.

Preheat the oil in a deep-fryer to 365° F.

Working in batches, add about a quarter of the strips to the hot oil and fry just until browned (about 1 minute). Remove with a skimmer or slotted spoon and drain well on paper towels. Sprinkle lightly with paprika and salt, and serve.

Reminder: Always prepare your ingredients, utensils and working area before starting to cook. Deep frying safely will demand your complete attention.

Remember never to fill your fryer more than half-full with oil.

Tofu Treats

4 servings

Tofu is an excellent source of protein. If you're not used to eating it, you might think it's bland, but—just like most foods—it tastes great deep-fried.

The blocks of tofu are packed in water and need to be well drained. Wrap the tofu in a thin cotton towel and press for an hour between weighted plates. This will squeeze out some of the moisture and prevent a great deal of hot oil splattering.

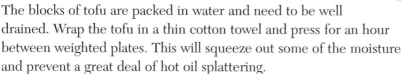

¼ cup soy sauce
½ teaspoon dark sesame oil
1 tablespoon dry sherry (optional)
1 teaspoon sugar
1 scallion, thinly sliced
½ cup water
1 pound firm tofu, drained, pressed and patted dry
Vegetable oil for deep frying

In a small bowl, combine the soy sauce, sesame oil, sherry, sugar and scallion. Add the water and stir to dissolve the sugar. Set aside as a dipping sauce.

Cut the tofu into 1-inch squares and pat dry once more.

Preheat the oil in a deep-fryer to 375° F.

Add about one-quarter of the tofu to the hot oil and cook until puffed and golden (about 3 minutes). If the tofu sticks to the bottom of the pot, stir it until it floats to the surface. Drain well on a paper-towel–lined tray, and repeat with the remaining tofu. Serve with the dipping sauce and chopsticks or toothpicks.

Remember never to fill your fryer more than half-full with oil.

❄ ✿ ○ ❧

Tasty Tempura

4 servings

This just might be the easiest way in the world to get the kids to eat their veggies.
Thin, even slices of many vegetables dipped in batter will fry up light and very crisp.
You may decide to leave out some vegetables or add others.

PREPARE THE VEGETABLES

With a sharp knife, cut the sweet potato into
¼-inch slices. Soak in a bowl of cold water for
10 minutes; drain and pat dry. Cut the
onion into thin slices. Prepare the other
vegetables as listed and set aside.

To prepare the shrimp, snip or score their under-
bellys with a few shallow cuts so they do not curl
when placed in the fryer.

Prepare a tray lined with sheets of paper towels to
drain the cooked tempura pieces.

Preheat the oil in a deep-fryer to 350° F.

PREPARE THE BATTER

In a large bowl, combine the flour, cornstarch and
baking soda. Pour in the club soda and whisk
together; do not whisk out all of the lumps. Use the
batter right away.

The Vegetables

1 small sweet potato, peeled
1 medium onion, peeled
4 scallions, trimmed to 3 inches
4 mushrooms, halved or sliced
8 string beans, ends trimmed
8 asparagus spears, peeled and trimmed to 3 inches
8 sugar-snap peas
1 carrot, halved crosswise, thinly sliced lengthwise
8 medium shrimp, peeled and de-veined

The Batter

1½ cups low gluten flour (biscuit, pastry or cake flour)
½ cup cornstarch
½ teaspoon baking soda
2 cups club soda

Vegetable oil for deep frying
Lemon wedges
Soy sauce

Working with one type of vegetable at a time (sweet potato, onion, scallions, mushrooms, string beans, asparagus, peas and carrot) dip the pieces, one at a time, into the batter and carefully drop them into the hot oil. Do not crowd the pan. Fry one batch for 2 minutes until crisp but still pale.

Transfer them to paper towels with a skimmer or slotted spoon. Skim bits of batter from the oil.

Repeat the process with the remaining batches. Serve hot, with lemon or a small bowl of soy sauce for dipping, as they do in Japan.

Remember never to fill your fryer more than half-full with oil.

Chinese Dumplings

4 to 6 servings

Chinese Dumplings can often be bought frozen. For an easy, quick-fix appetizer, buy them ready-made or substitute frozen filled wontons. Make sure they are defrosted slowly and patted dry before frying.

If you are making your own dumplings, fresh or frozen dumpling skins and wonton wrappers (Chinese), or the thinner and more delicate gyoza skins (Japanese), are available in most supermarkets. You can also cut out your own wrappers from thinly rolled-out sheets of fresh pasta.

PREPARE THE DUMPLINGS

In a large bowl, stir together the soy sauce, sherry, sesame oil and cornstarch. Break up the meat into bits and sprinkle over the cornstarch mixture.

Spread the spinach, scallions, celery, garlic, salt and pepper over the meat and stir together with a fork.

Spread out 6 of the dumpling skins and set a teaspoon of filling on each one. Moisten around the edges and fold over the skin to enclose the filling. Push out any air bubbles and press to seal the sides. Refrigerate the filled dumplings and repeat with the remaining ingredients.

The Dumplings

- 1 tablespoon soy sauce
- 1 tablespoon dry sherry
- 2 teaspoons dark sesame oil
- 2 teaspoons cornstarch
- 12 ounces ground pork, chicken or turkey
- ½ box chopped frozen spinach, defrosted, tightly squeezed and chopped again
- 3 scallions, trimmed and minced
- 1 celery stalk, minced
- 2 garlic cloves, minced
- 1 teaspoon salt
- ½ teaspoon pepper
- 1 12- to 16-ounce package dumpling skins, wonton wrappers or gyoza skins
  Vegetable oil for deep frying

The Dipping Sauce

- ½ cup soy sauce
- 1 teaspoon dark sesame oil
- 1 teaspoon dry sherry
- ½ teaspoon sugar
- 1 crushed garlic clove

PREPARE THE DIPPING SAUCE

Add all of the ingredients to a jar; cover and shake well. Pour into a small bowl.

Spread paper towels on a tray for draining the fried dumplings.

Preheat oil in a deep-fryer to 365° F. Fry the dumplings, 6 at a time, until golden brown (about 4 minutes). With a skimmer, carefully transfer the dumplings to the paper towels to drain.

After draining, spread the dumplings out on a wire rack and keep them warm in an oven at low heat while you repeat the frying process with the remaining batches.

Serve with the dipping sauce.

Remember never to fill your fryer more than half-full with oil.

Stuffed Green Chiles

4 to 6 servings

Also known as Chiles Rellenos, these chiles are simply stuffed with cheese, dipped in batter and fried; however, they can also be stuffed with a mixture of cooked chopped meat and onions. You can buy cans of ready-peeled chiles, but the best-tasting kind are the ones you blanch and peel yourself.

We've also included an easy recipe for your own home-made sauce, but canned chili sauce will work, too.

The Batter
- 1 cup cornmeal
- ⅔ cup all-purpose flour
- 1 teaspoon baking powder
- ½ teaspoon salt
- 2 eggs
- 1 cup milk

Preheat your broiler or barbecue grill to a moderately high temperature. Spread the chiles in a single layer and cook them, turning each one with a pair of tongs until they are blistered all over, which happens fairly quickly. (A bit of charring improves the flavor.) Be sure to blister them evenly so that the skins can be easily peeled off. Drop the chiles into a bowl of ice-cold water to loosen the skins. With your fingers, pull off the skins. Cut the chiles open with a lengthwise slit and scrape out the seeds and ribs with the blunt edge of a knife. Rinse the chiles and pat them dry.

Cut the cheese into 12 strips and place one inside each chile and close the slit.

PREPARE THE BATTER

In a bowl, stir together the cornmeal, flour, baking

The Chile Sauce
1 tablespoon vegetable oil
1 medium onion, finely chopped
2 garlic cloves, minced
¼ cup mild or hot chili powder
1 28-ounce can chopped tomatoes
1 8-ounce can tomato sauce
Salt
Vegetable oil for deep frying

powder and salt. Make a well in the center, add the eggs and milk and whisk to a smooth batter. Set the batter aside while you make the chile sauce.

PREPARE THE CHILE SAUCE

In a sucepan, heat the oil and cook the onion over moderate heat until soft but not browned (about 5 minutes). Stir in the garlic and cook for 1 minute. Stir in the chili powder and cook for 2 minutes. Stir in the tomatoes and tomato sauce and bring to a gentle boil. Cook, stirring now and then, for 10 minutes. Add salt to taste.

Preheat the oil in a deep-fryer to 375° F. Working in batches, dip the chiles in the batter and carefully lower them into the hot oil. Fry until golden all over and drain well on paper towels, using a skimmer or slotted spoon to transfer the chiles. Serve the chiles hot with the chile sauce and some grits on the side, if desired.

Remember never to fill your fryer more than half-full with oil.

Buffalo Chicken Wings

5 to 6 servings

Everyone knows that roasted chicken wings always hit the spot. Now try them deep-fried and enjoy them a new way with this familiar, blue cheese dip.

The Buffalo Dip
- 8 ounces blue cheese, crumbled
- 1 cup thick mayonnaise
- ⅔ cup sour cream
- 1 tablespoon fresh lemon juice
- 1 teaspoon Worcestershire sauce
- ¼ teaspoon cayenne pepper
- ¼ teaspoon onion powder or garlic powder

- 2 pounds chicken wings
  Vegetable oil for deep frying
  Hot pepper sauce

In a bowl, using a fork, mash three-quarters of the cheese. Blend in the mayonnaise, sour cream, lemon juice, Worcestershire sauce, cayenne pepper and onion or garlic powder. Stir in the rest of the cheese.

Cut the wing tips from the chicken and discard them. Cut the wings in half at the joints. Wash and dry the chicken wings.

Preheat the oil in a deep-fryer to 375° F. Add the wings to the hot oil and cook until golden brown (about 15 minutes). Drain well and serve with the dip, a bottle of hot pepper sauce and plenty of napkins.

Remember never to fill your fryer more than half-full with oil.

Crispy Onion Rings

4 servings

These are a classic sidedish for hamburgers, steak or fried chicken. They are also an excellent snack for everyday nibbling.

  2 cups all-purpose flour
½ cup cornstarch
  1 teaspoon salt
¼ teaspoon pepper
1½ cups club soda
  4 onions, peeled and sliced across the stem, ¼ inch thick
     Vegetable oil for deep frying

In a large bowl, combine 1 cup of the flour with the cornstarch, salt and pepper. Pour in all of the club soda and stir with a wire whisk until smoothly blended. Cover and refrigerate until cold (about an hour).

Separate the onion slices into rings, and put the remaining flour in a plastic bag.

Preheat the oil in a deep-fryer to 370° F.

Drop the onion rings into the bag of flour and shake.

Stir the batter.

With a long, pronged fork, dip the rings, a few at a time, into the batter and carefully drop them into the hot oil. Fry in small batches until golden (about 1 minute). Drain on paper towels. Sprinkle with salt and serve immediately.

Remember never to fill your fryer more than half-full with oil.

Tempura Pecans

Makes ½ pound

When you bite into these tasty snacks, you'll get a charge from the tempura crust crackling in your mouth. For an interesting twist, you may include 1 teaspoon of fresh herbs such as marjoram, thyme or rosemary. You may also substitute walnuts, almonds or hazelnuts for the pecans.

½ cup rice flour
½ cup seltzer water
½ teaspoon salt
½ pound roasted unsalted pecans
Vegetable shortening for deep frying

In a small bowl, mix together rice flour, seltzer and salt. Coat the pecans in the batter, then place in a colander to allow excess to drip off.

Preheat the shortening in a deep-fryer to 375° F.

Carefully drop the nuts into the hot oil by the handful, separating them as you drop them in so they do not clump.

Fry until the bubbles subside (about 2 minutes). Serve hot.

Remember never to fill your fryer more than half-full with oil.

Camembert Fried in Beer Batter

8 servings

Cheese and jam may sound like an unusual combination, but it is actually quite delicious. Crunchy batter, tangy Camembert and sweet or tart jam hit all the right taste notes at once.

Follow up this dish with a crisp green salad for a perfect brunch or lunch.

The Batter
- 2 cups all-purpose flour
- 1 cup beer at room temperature
- 2 tablespoons vegetable oil
- 2 large eggs, beaten

- All-purpose flour, as needed
- 32 ounces Camembert cheese, cut into 16 pieces
- Vegetable oil for deep frying
- Strawberry or raspberry jam

Put flour in a medium bowl. In another bowl, whisk together beer, 2 tablespoons oil and eggs. Make a well in the center of the flour and pour in egg mixture. Beat until smooth. Cover and refrigerate at least 2 hours and up to 24 hours.

Preheat the oil in a deep-fryer to 375° F.

Roll cheese pieces in flour, patting off excess. Dip them in the batter and carefully fry in batches until brown and crisp. Using a fryer basket, drain and transfer to paper towels. Serve hot with strawberry or raspberry jam for dipping.

Remember never to fill your fryer more than half-full with oil.

Chinese-Style Shrimp Puffs

4 to 6 servings

If you like shrimp toast, you will love these super-easy-to-make shrimp puffs. Serve them with "duck" sauce—A.K.A. sweet-and-sour sauce—and spicy Chinese mustard.

1 pound peeled, de-veined raw shrimp
3 scallions, trimmed and cut into 1-inch pieces
2 large eggs
2 teaspoons cornstarch
1 teaspoon chopped fresh ginger
½ teaspoon salt
½ cup breadcrumbs
Vegetable oil for deep frying

Combine the shrimp, scallions, eggs, cornstarch, ginger and salt in a food processor. Purée until smooth.

Spread the breadcrumbs on a shallow plate. Scoop heaping teaspoons of the shrimp mixture onto the breadcrumbs and gently roll into balls.

Preheat the oil in a deep-fryer to 375° F.

Carefully drop the balls into the hot oil, no more than 8 at a time, and fry until golden (4 to 6 minutes), turning once. Remove the shrimp puffs with a skimmer, drain and transfer to paper towels. Repeat with the remaining batter. Serve warm.

Remember never to fill your fryer more than half-full with oil.

Fried Mozzarella Sticks

6 to 8 servings

Even though you might think that fresh mozzarella would be better for this recipe, unfortunately it is too wet. Stick to the store-bought variety, and you will be happy with the results. The secret to keeping the cheese from leaking out is to make sure that the mozzarella stick is fully coated with breadcrumbs. Don't miss a spot. The secret to the great flavor is the Oklahoma Joe's™ BBQ sauce!

1 pound mozzarella
½ cup flour
2 eggs
1½ cups breadcrumbs
1 teaspoon salt
½ teaspoon ground black pepper
Vegetable oil for deep frying
Oklahoma Joe's™ BBQ sauce

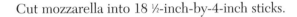

Cut mozzarella into 18 ½-inch-by-4-inch sticks.

Spread flour in a shallow dish. Lightly beat eggs and place in another shallow dish. Combine breadcrumbs, salt and pepper in another shallow dish.

Dredge cheese sticks in the flour until completely coated. Shake off excess. One at a time, dip them in the egg then in the breadcrumb mixture. Dip again in egg and then again in breadcrumb mixture.

Preheat the oil in a deep-fryer to 375° F.

Place a layer of mozzarella sticks in a fryer basket. Carefully lower it into the hot oil and fry the sticks until they are golden (about 1 minute). Remove the fryer basket, drain and transfer the mozzarella sticks to paper towels. Repeat with the remaining mozzarella. Serve with Oklahoma Joe's™ BBQ sauce.

Remember never to fill your fryer more than half-full with oil.

Deep-Fried Spring Rolls

Makes about 30 rolls

These spring rolls can be served with a plate of red leaf lettuce, mint and basil. Guests wrap the fried rolls in the leaves to eat them. You can also make them up to 2 weeks in advance and keep them in the freezer, uncooked.

The Spring Rolls
- 1 ounce bean thread vermicelli
- 1 tablespoon crumbled dried mushrooms (such as wood ear or shittake)
- 2 eggs
- 1 clove garlic, minced
- 1 tablespoon grated ginger
- ¼ cup finely sliced scallion
- ½ teaspoon salt
- ¼ teaspoon pepper
- 1 teaspoon sugar
- 1½ teaspoon sesame oil
- 2 tablespoon chopped cilantro
- ½ pound ground pork
- ¼ cup grated carrot
- 1 package wonton skins (defrosted if frozen
- 1 head red leaf lettuce
- 1 cup basil leaves
- 1 cup mint leaves

PREPARE THE SPRING ROLLS

In a small bowl pour boiling water over the vermicelli and mushrooms—enough to cover them—and seal off the bowl with a lid; let stand for 30 minutes. Drain by pulling the vermicelli and mushrooms out of the water with pasta tongs, leaving any sediment behind.

In a large bowl, whisk together 1 egg, the garlic, ginger, scallion, salt, pepper, sugar, sesame oil and cilantro. Stir in the pork, carrot and vermicelli mixture until well combined.

In a small bowl, beat remaining egg, then set aside. Loosely cover the wonton skins in plastic wrap.

On a clean surface, lay 1 wonton skin with a corner facing you. Keep the remaining skins covered. Paint the edges of the skin with the egg wash. Place a heaping teaspoon of the filling on the corner facing you. Roll the bottom corner toward the middle 1 turn, so that the filling is completely encased. Fold in the other corners and finish the roll. Set aside on a baking sheet.

Vegetable shortening for deep frying

The Dipping Sauce
½ cup soy sauce
½ cup lime juice
2 tablespoons water
1 large clove garlic, minced to a paste
2 tablespoons sugar
1 small red chili pepper, minced
1 scallion, thinly sliced

Combine all the dipping sauce ingredients in a small bowl. Stir until combined and sugar is dissolved.

Repeat until you have used all the filling. You may make the recipe up to this point and freeze the rolls in an airtight container for up to 2 weeks.

Preheat the shortening in a deep-fryer to 375° F.

Fry, in single layer batches, until golden (about 5 minutes). Be sure to allow the rolls enough room to fit comfortably without sticking to each other. Remove to a paper-towel–lined sheet pan for draining. Serve with the dipping sauce and a plate of lettuce, mint and basil.

Remember never to fill your fryer more than half-full with oil.

Cornmeal-Crusted Jalapeño Poppers

4 servings

These southwestern bar favorites are easier to make than you might imagine. But if you bite into an especially spicy one, they can be hotter than you ever dreamed. Be sure to have a stash of cold beer, cold milk or bread nearby when you serve them.

The Coating
- ½ cup corn meal
- ¼ cup flour
- 1 tablespoon Oklahoma Joe's™ Original BBQ seasoning
- ¼ teaspoon ground black pepper

PREPARE THE COATING

Combine corn meal, flour, Oklahoma Joe's™ Original BBQ seasoning and ground black pepper in a shallow dish.

PREPARE THE PEPPERS

With a small, sharp knife, cut a slit from the stem to the tip of each pepper. Using the point of the knife, carefully scrape out the seeds and the membrane without breaking the pepper apart.

Stuff each jalapeño with about 1 tablespoon of the cheese. Don't overstuff the peppers. You want them to be able to close.

Place the flour in a shallow dish. Lightly beat the egg and place it in another shallow dish. One at a time, dredge the peppers in the flour; shake off excess. Then dip them in the beaten egg, then dredge in the cornmeal coating.

Tips:

When working with jalapeños or other hot peppers, it is a good idea to wear rubber gloves or protect your hands by keeping them in plastic bags. Touching a powerfully hot pepper can make your hands, as well as anything you touch, burn for days.

Jalapeños vary in spiciness, even within the same batch. So remember, just because the last one you ate was mild doesn't mean that the next one won't be devilishly hot.

The Peppers
12 jalapeño peppers
¾ cup shredded Monterey Jack cheese
½ cup flour
1 egg
Vegetable oil for deep frying

Preheat the oil in a deep fryer to 375° F.

Carefully drop the peppers into the oil, watching for splatters, and fry until golden (about 3 minutes). Remove with fryer basket, drain and transfer peppers to paper towels. Serve immediately.

Remember never to fill your fryer more than half-full with oil.

Four-Cheese Croquettes

Makes 18

Feel free to vary the cheeses when making croquettes. Croquettes provide the perfect opportunity to use odds and ends from the fridge—in fact, that is what makes them fun to prepare. You may also want to add some minced onion or herbs, if you have any on hand.

3 ounces Fontina, grated
3 ounces Gorgonzola, or other blue cheese, crumbled
6 ounces Parmesan, grated
2 ounces Emmenthaler, or other strong Swiss-style cheese, grated
2 large eggs, beaten
½ teaspoon nutmeg
Fine, dry breadcrumbs, as needed
Vegetable oil for deep frying

In a medium bowl, blend together cheeses, eggs and nutmeg. Cover and refrigerate for 3 or 4 hours, or overnight.

Put breadcrumbs into a shallow bowl. Divide cheese mixture into 18 pieces and roll into balls. Roll the balls in breadcrumbs to coat completely, pressing the crumbs onto the croquettes.

Preheat the oil in a deep-fryer to 375° F.

Fry croquettes in small batches until evenly browned (about 3 minutes). Using fryer basket, drain and transfer to paper towels. Serve hot.

Remember never to fill your fryer more than half-full with oil.

Portobello Mushrooms in Wine Batter

4 to 6 servings

These mushrooms are available year-round. They have a strong, rich flavor and can satisfy even the most hardcore meat lovers.

1 pound portobello mushrooms, stems removed
  Pepper
1 cup all-purpose flour
½ cup cornstarch
1 teaspoon salt
1 egg
1¼ cups dry white wine
  Vegetable oil for deep frying
  Soy sauce (optional)

Rinse the mushrooms under cold running water and pat dry. Mushrooms up to 3 inches in diameter can be cooked whole. If they are larger, remove some of the black gills by scooping them out with a teaspoon or knife, Cut in half and then slice both pieces into half-inch wide strips. Season the mushrooms with pepper.

In a large bowl, mix together the flour, cornstarch and salt. Add the egg and all of the wine and whisk together until smooth. Cover and let sit about 1 hour.

Preheat the oil in a deep-fryer to 365° F.

Spread sheets of paper towels on a tray for draining.

Dip the pieces in the batter and fry them in batches until the batter is golden (about 5 minutes per batch). Drain well and serve hot with soy sauce if desired.

Remember never to fill your fryer more than half-full with oil.

Onion Blossoms

4 servings

Deep-fried onion blossoms, sometimes called onion chrysanthemums, have become extremely popular restaurant fare. They seem very difficult to make, but in reality, they're quite easy. (The only hard part is keeping yourself from eating too much!)

The Dipping Sauce
- ½ cup sour cream
- 1 tsp Oklahoma Joe's™ Sweet & Spicy seasoning

The Onions
- 2 large, sweet white onions
- ⅔ cup flour
- 3 tablespoons cornstarch
- 1 teaspoon salt
- 1 egg
- 2 tablespoons water
- Vegetable oil for deep frying

PREPARE THE DIPPING SAUCE

Stir together sour cream and Oklahoma Joe's™ Sweet & Spicy seasoning. Refrigerate 30 minutes or until ready to serve.

PREPARE THE ONIONS

Peel onions and trim the top and root ends. Cut onions into blossom shape by one of the methods in the Tips box on the next page. Place onion in a dish of water and microwave until water is steaming. Set aside until water is cool. Separate onion layers to form blossom shape. Pat dry.

In a small bowl, blend together flour, cornstarch and salt. In a shallow bowl, beat egg with water.

Toss onion blossoms with flour mixture, then dip top of "leaves" into egg mixture and sprinkle liberally with more of the flour mixture.

Preheat the oil in a deep-fryer to 365° F.

Tips:

There are 3 ways that you can cut an onion into a blossom shape.
Place the onion, root end down, on the work surface.

METHOD #1
Using a sharp knife, cut the onion from top to bottom almost all the way through. Then make a perpendicular cut, again almost all the way through. Make two more cuts, like pie slices, through the center of the onion (again, not all the way through) to form 8 segments.

METHOD #2
Using an apple corer/sectioner, position the corer on top of the onion and press down, making sure that you don't cut all the way through. To use this method, you must peel away enough layers of the onion to make sure that it fits through the corer.

METHOD #3
You can purchase an apple blossom maker at discount stores and through TV offers.

Place one onion blossom in a fryer basket. Lower into the hot oil and fry until golden (about 4 minutes). Remove fryer basket, drain and transfer onion blossom to paper towels. Repeat with second onion. Serve warm with the dipping sauce.

Remember never to fill your fryer more than half-full with oil.

Fresh Tortilla Chips

4 to 6 servings

Now you can have the freshest corn chips available anywhere. Serve them as everyday munchies, or set them in a basket alongside bowls of salsa and guacamole and watch how fast your guests make them disappear.

12 fresh corn tortillas
Vegetable oil for deep frying
Salt
Salsa (optional)
Guacamole (optional)

Stack the tortillas in 2 piles and cut through the stacks with a sharp, heavy knife to make small triangles—you should be able to make 12 per tortilla. You can also cut each tortilla with a pair of scissors.

Separate the triangles so they are not stuck together, and let them air dry while you prepare the oil and a tray lined with paper towels for draining the chips.

Preheat the oil in a deep-fryer to 375° F. Carefully add a layer of chips to the hot oil and fry, stirring once or twice with a slotted spoon. Transfer to the paper towels as soon as they are golden and crisp, sprinkle with salt and repeat with the remaining chips. Serve warm or at room temperature with salsa and guacamole, if desired.

Remember never to fill your fryer more than half-full with oil.

Poultry

Deep-Fried Turkey

12 to 15 servings

This is a dramatic way to cook America's favorite holiday bird. More importantly, a deep-fried turkey has moist, flavorful, grease-free meat and crisp, tasty skin. The turkey will cook in a very short time, only 3½ minutes per pound. Thus, a 12- to 15-pound bird will cook in under an hour.

It takes a big pot and 3 gallons of oil to cover a bird of this size. Our recipe uses a New Braunfels 26-quart deep-fryer and calls for Oklahoma Joe's™ Turkey Fry Oil.

Keep in mind that it takes a fairly strong and steady arm to slowly lower a turkey into hot oil, and then, when it is cooked, to carefully raise it out. Cover yourself sensibly with long sleeves, pants and closed-toe shoes when deep-frying.

3 gallons Oklahoma Joe's™ Turkey Fry Oil
1 packet Oklahoma Joe's™ Zesty Marinade mix
1 turkey, 12 to 15 pounds, patted dry

Set a rack in a large baking pan nearby, so you can stand the cooked turkey on the rack for draining.

If you are using a frozen turkey, make sure that it has defrosted slowly and thoroughly—if it is chilled, it will lower the oil temperature too much—and remove any packages of gizzards from inside. Use plenty of paper towels to pat the bird as dry as possible, both inside and out; this step greatly reduces splattering when the turkey is added to the oil.

Shake up the marinade mix in a jar. Using an injector, inject the marinade deeply into the thick areas of the turkey breast and thighs. Slowly withdraw the injector as you squeeze to evenly distribute the marinade.

Preheat the oil in a deep-fryer to 325° F.

Insert the star-shaped fry accessory into the turkey cavity, so that the legs of the bird are at the top. (Unlike our illustration, which shows the opposite configuration!) This stand will prevent the base of the turkey from touching the bottom of the pot and enable you to safely manuever it into and out of the hot oil.

Use the lift handle to hook onto the top of the turkey fry accessory. Lower the turkey very, very slowly into the hot oil. When the oil bubbles up, pause and wait for a few seconds until it subsides before continuing to lower the turkey to the base of the fryer. The oil temperature will drop immediately, so raise the heat to full power, but begin timing the turkey immediately.

Check the oil temperature every 10 minutes or so. As soon as it reaches 325° F. again, lower the heat just enough to maintain that temperature for the remainder of the calculated cooking time.

Using the lift handle again, remove the turkey from the oil and set on the prepared rack. With a meat thermometer, check the temperature of the thickest section of the breast and thigh. It should be about 180° F.

When the turkey has cooled slightly, remove the accessory from the cavity and let the juices settle for 15 minutes before carving.

Remember never to fill your fryer more than half-full with oil.

Soy-and-Garlic Fried Turkey Drumsticks

6 servings

The soy-and-garlic marinade gives the turkey a delicious, distinct, smoky flavor.

Unlike most fried foods, this one will keep extremely well in the refrigerator for a couple of days, so you can use it for sandwiches later.

7 large cloves garlic, finely chopped
2 teaspoons grated ginger (optional)
2 cups soy sauce
6 turkey drumsticks
  Vegetable shortening for deep frying

In a large resealable plastic bag, combine garlic, ginger and soy sauce. Add the turkey drumsticks. Squeeze out the air, seal the bag and marinate for at least 4 hours or overnight.

Preheat the shortening in a deep-fryer to 400° F.

Remove from plastic bag and fry the turkey legs until the internal temperature registers 165° F. on an instant-read thermometer (about 12 minutes). By this time, the drumsticks should be a deep golden in color. Serve with cranberry sauce and Apple Doughnuts (p. 169) for a crisp and classic autumn meal.

Remember never to fill your fryer more than half-full with oil.

Crispy Fried Chicken Fingers

4 servings

These classic fried chicken fingers will please kids and grown-ups alike. No bones about it.

1 pound chicken tenders
1 cup flour
5 teaspoons Oklahoma Joe's™ Steak seasoning
¾ teaspoon salt
½ teaspoon ground black pepper
1 egg
2 tablespoons milk
Vegetable oil for deep frying

Pat chicken tenders dry with paper towels. Combine flour, Oklahoma Joe's™ Steak seasoning, salt and pepper in a large bowl. Lightly beat egg with milk in a small bowl.

Toss chicken tenders with flour until well coated. Remove from flour. One at a time, dip tenders into egg, and then dredge well in flour mixture again.

Preheat the oil in a deep-fryer to 365° F.

Place half the chicken tenders in a fryer basket. Lower into the hot oil and fry until golden (3 to 4 minutes). Remove the fryer basket, drain and transfer to paper towels. Repeat with remaining chicken tenders. Serve with one of the many dipping sauces in this book (pages 29, 33 or 48).

Remember never to fill your fryer more than half-full with oil.

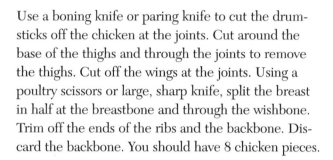

Southern Fried Chicken

4 to 6 servings

1 3- to 4-pound chicken
1 cup buttermilk
1 cup all-purpose flour
1 tablespoon salt
1 teaspoon freshly ground
  black pepper
½ teaspoon cayenne
  Vegetable oil for deep frying

Use a boning knife or paring knife to cut the drumsticks off the chicken at the joints. Cut around the base of the thighs and through the joints to remove the thighs. Cut off the wings at the joints. Using a poultry scissors or large, sharp knife, split the breast in half at the breastbone and through the wishbone. Trim off the ends of the ribs and the backbone. Discard the backbone. You should have 8 chicken pieces.

Put the chicken pieces into a shallow bowl and pour the buttermilk over them. Turn the chicken to coat all sides.

Put the flour, salt, pepper and cayenne into a large, brown paper bag, close it and shake to mix the flour and seasonings.

Cover a sheetpan or large plate with paper towels to use for draining the chicken after it has been fried.

Preheat the oil in a deep-fryer to 375° F.

Take the chicken out of the buttermilk and let the excess drip off. Put all the chicken into the bag of flour and shake it to coat the chicken completely.

First put the legs and thighs into the oil. They should sizzle loudly. Cover the fryer partially and let the chicken cook until it is nicely browned (about 5 minutes). Use long tongs to turn the chicken pieces.

Tips:

When frying chicken, it is very important not to crowd the oil. If too much chicken is added at once, the oil will cool too much and the crust on the chicken will not become crisp.

Never use a fork to turn chicken when it is frying. The fork will pierce the chicken and allow the delicious juices to run out.

For extra flavor, try adding a chunk of butter or a piece of smoked pork to the frying oil for the last five minutes of frying. If you add butter, the chicken will be a tiny bit less crispy but will have that irresistible butter flavor as compensation. If you add smoked pork, it will infuse your fried chicken with a subtle smoky taste. Be sure to discard the oil if you do add butter or pork.

If you are looking for a healthier version of fried chicken, you may remove the skin before dipping in buttermilk and flour, or you may substitute eight skinless chicken breasts for the eight chicken pieces. If using all breast meat, cook the chicken for 25 minutes only, or it will be dry and overcooked.

Add the remaining chicken to the fryer and let it brown also (about 5 minutes). Turn the chicken pieces over and reduce the temperature on the fryer to 325° F. Fry the chicken for an additional 20 minutes, turning the pieces once or twice to be sure that they brown evenly. Using a fryer basket, drain and transfer to paper-towel–lined sheetpan. Serve hot, at room temperature or cold.

Remember never to fill your fryer more than half-full with oil.

Cocoa-Covered Country Quail

4 servings (2 birds per person)

Because of its tangy spice rub, this quail dish comes out with a slightly barbecued flavor. If the high-quality cocoa powders listed below are not available at your local supermarket, good old Hershey's will work as well. You can also try this recipe with other upland game birds.

½ cup plus 2 tablespoons high-quality dark cocoa powder, such as Droste or Valrhona
2 teaspoons ground ginger
2 teaspoons dried oregano
½ teaspoon ancho or other chili powder
½ teaspoon salt
⅛ teaspoon pepper
8 quail, cleaned, rinsed and patted dry
Vegetable shortening for deep frying

In a small bowl, whisk together all dry ingredients.

Sprinkle about ½ teaspoon of the mixture inside each bird, then sprinkle the birds' whole bodies with the remainder of the mixture, being sure to cover each bird completely.

Place the seasoned quail on a sheet pan and wrap in plastic. Refrigerate for 8 hours or overnight.

When the birds are good and cold, and you're ready to cook them, preheat the shortening in a deep-fryer to 375° F.

Arrange a tray lined with paper towels for draining the cooked birds.

Remove the quail from the refrigerator and, using

a dry pastry brush, brush off any excess seasoning. Carefully place the birds in the deep-fryer with a pair of tongs.

Fry the birds in batches of 4 for 5 minutes. Remove them with the tongs to the paper towels.

Serve them with Bright-Green Parsley Garnish (p. 108) and Deep-Fried Squash Blossoms (p. 22) from your own garden for a meal that makes the most of the great outdoors.

Remember never to fill your fryer more than half-full with oil.

Cornish Hens with Asian Spices

2 servings

Spice rubs add delicious flavor to deep-fried birds; as an alternative to this Asian blend, use a few tablespoons of curry or chili powder. To serve four, double the spice mix and cook the hens two at a time, keeping the first batch warm in a low-temperature oven while the last ones fry.

2 teaspoons ground ginger
2 teaspoons ground black pepper
2 teaspoons anise seeds, crushed
2 teaspoons salt
1 teaspoon ground cinnamon
1 teaspoon ground cloves
½ teaspoon cayenne pepper
2 Cornish hens, about 1¾ pounds each
Vegetable oil for deep frying

In a small bowl, mix ginger, black pepper, anise seeds, salt, cinnamon, cloves and cayenne pepper.

Rinse the hens inside and out, and pat dry with paper towels. Pull off and discard any excess fat. Rub the spice mixture all over the outside of the hens, and sprinkle some into the interior cavity.

Preheat the oil in a deep-fryer to 375° F. Carefully add the hens 1 at a time to the hot oil with tongs.

Cook the hens until they are deeply brown (10 to 12 minutes). To check for doneness, lift one of the hens out of the oil and insert an instant-read thermometer into the thickest part of the breast—it should read 170° F. Serve with Wonton Nibbles (p. 28) for a pan-Asian meal!

Remember never to fill your fryer more than half-full with oil.

Lemon-Sesame Chicken Breasts

6 servings

6 boneless, skinless chicken
  breast halves
1 cup buttermilk
2 tablespoons fresh lemon juice
2 cloves garlic, minced
1 cup unseasoned dry
  breadcrumbs
½ cup sesame seeds
¼ cup freshly grated
  Parmesan cheese
  Vegetable oil for deep frying

Place chicken breast halves between 2 sheets of plastic wrap; pound with a heavy pan or rolling pin to flatten into a more even layer.

In a shallow dish, combine buttermilk, lemon juice and garlic; add the chicken, turning to coat. Cover and refrigerate at least 4 hours or overnight.

Preheat the oil in a deep-fryer to 350° F.

In a small bowl, combine breadcrumbs, sesame seeds and cheese. Remove the chicken from the buttermilk, shaking off the excess. Press both sides of each chicken breast firmly in the breadcrumb mixture to coat well.

Carefully add 3 of the breasts to the oil, one at a time (the oil will bubble up). Cook until golden on the outside and no longer pink in the center (about 2 minutes). Set aside to keep warm while you fry the remaining 3 breasts. Season with salt and pepper.

Remember never to fill your fryer more than half-full with oil.

Chicken in Beer Batter

4 servings

A good batter should sit for an hour before being used, so plan ahead. Cornstarch gives the batter a nice crunch.

The Beer Batter
1⅓ cups all-purpose flour
⅓ cup cornstarch
1 tablespoon Oklahoma Joe's™ Hog Rub & Yard Bird seasoning
1 teaspoon salt
¼ teaspoon pepper
1 cold 12-ounce beer

The Chicken
1 cup all-purpose flour
1 teaspoon salt
½ teaspoon pepper
1 chicken, about 3 pounds, cut into 8 pieces
Vegetable oil for deep frying

PREPARE THE BEER BATTER

In a large bowl, combine flour, cornstarch, seasoning, salt and pepper. Pour in all of the beer and stir briskly with a wire whisk until smoothly blended. Cover and refrigerate until cold (about 1 hour).

PREPARE THE CHICKEN

Preheat the oil in a deep-fryer to 375° F.

In a large plastic bag, toss together flour, salt and pepper. Add 4 pieces of chicken to the bag and shake well.

Stir the Beer Batter. Dip floured chicken into batter and lower with tongs into the hot oil. Fry until golden, about 12 minutes. Using fryer basket, drain and transfer chicken to paper towels. Repeat with remaining chicken.

Serve warm with Perfect Boiled Corn (p. 147).

Remember never to fill your fryer more than half-full with oil.

Meats

❄ ✿ ☼ 🍂

Chicken Fried Steak with Milk Gravy

4 servings

Chicken Fried Steak has always been a favorite down-home recipe and a standard menu item in most soul-food restaurants. The secret is in its simplicity—and now you can enjoy this quick, easy dish any time of year, in the comfort of your own home.

The Steaks
- 2 eggs
- 1 cup all-purpose flour
- 2 tablespoons kosher salt
- ½ teaspoon freshly ground black pepper
- ⅛ teaspoon cayenne
- 4 6-ounce steaks (sirloin or round), tenderized with a mallet and pounded to ¼-inch thin
- Vegetable shortening for deep frying

PREPARE THE FILLETS

In a small bowl, beat the eggs. Pour egg mixture onto a large plate. On a separate large plate, combine flour, salt, black pepper and cayenne.

Heat the shortening in a deep-fryer to 350° F.

Working with one fillet at a time, coat in egg, allowing excess liquid to drip off. Toss steak in the flour mixture, shaking off any excess, then coat in egg again. Place the coated fillets on a sheet pan. Repeat until all the fillets have been coated.

Carefully place the fillets in the deep-fryer with a pair of tongs. Fry them until lightly golden (about 4 minutes). Remove the fillets with the tongs and transfer them to a paper-towel–lined sheet pan for draining.

Serve hot with the milk gravy and the Biscuits in Honey Glaze (p. 10).

The Milk Gravy

2 tablespoons melted bacon fat,
   butter or shortening
2 tablespoons all-purpose flour
4 cups of milk
   Salt and freshly ground pepper,
   to taste

PREPARE THE MILK GRAVY

In a heavy non-reactive sauce pan, whisk fat and flour together over low heat until the mixture is simmering. Gradually add the milk and bring to a simmer over high heat. Simmer, whisking constantly, until sauce is reduced by half (about 10 minutes). Season with salt and pepper.

Remember never to fill your fryer more than half-full with oil.

Breaded Pork Chops

4 to 8 servings

Allow one chop per person if other kinds of meat dishes are also being served.

Scrape the bone clean before frying, so it can be held with a napkin for nibbling.

8 thin center-cut pork chops
Salt
Pepper
3 tablespoons flour
1 tablespoon Oklahoma Joe's™
Hog Rub & Yard Bird seasoning
2 eggs
1 cup dried breadcrumbs
Vegetable oil for deep frying
Dijon-style mustard
Unsweetened applesauce

Pat the chops dry, and with a sharp knife or pair of scissors, make a few short cuts into the edge of the meat to prevent curling as it fries. Rub the pork all over with salt and pepper. Sprinkle the chops with flour and seasoning and shake off the excess.

Beat the eggs in a deep plate or shallow bowl, and spread the breadcrumbs on a plate near the eggs.

Holding a chop by the rib bone, dip it on both sides into the egg and let the excess egg drip back into the plate or bowl. Coat the chop with the breadcrumbs, and repeat with the rest of the chops.

Preheat the oil in a deep-fryer to 365° F. With tongs, carefully place the chops in the hot oil and cook them 4 at a time until golden and crisp (about 2 minutes). Remove, and drain well on paper towels.

Serve hot, with mustard and applesauce.

Remember never to fill your fryer more than half-full with oil.

Oklahoma Joe's™ Sizzlin' Steak

4 to 6 servings

Serve this dish with coleslaw and potato salad.

2 pounds lean, boneless sirloin
    steak, trimmed
4 tablespoons Oklahoma Joe's™
    Steak seasoning
2 tablespoons cornstarch
    Vegetable oil for deep frying

Sprinkle the steak all over with Oklahoma Joe's™ Steak seasoning. Wrap the steak in plastic and refrigerate for 2 hours or overnight.

Preheat the oil in a deep-fryer to 330° F.

Wipe the steak dry and rub it all over with the cornstarch.

Carefully lower the steak into the hot oil and cook for 4 minutes per pound. Remove with tongs to a cutting board and let rest for 10 minutes. Slice thinly across the grain and serve.

Remember never to fill your fryer more than half-full with oil.

BBQ-Style Fried Beef Ribs

4 servings

Just as there are distinctions between "cake people" and "frosting people," there are distinctions between "meat people" and "bone people." The meat people prefer to slice up their steak and eat it bite by bite with a fork. The bone people, on the other hand, dutifully eat the meat only so that they can get to the bone, which they can pick up in their fingers to gnaw the juiciest, most luscious part of the meat from the rib. This recipe is for the bone people!

4 pounds beef ribs, about 8 ribs
3 tablespoons Oklahoma Joe's™ Original BBQ seasoning
¾ cup Oklahoma Joe's™ Barbecue Sauce

PREPARE THE RIBS

Rub the beef ribs with Oklahoma Joe's™ Original BBQ seasoning until they are completely coated.

Preheat the oil in a deep-fryer to 360° F.

One at a time, slowly lower the ribs into the hot oil. Fry them until they are well cooked (about 8 minutes). Carefully remove the ribs, drain and transfer to paper towels. Immediately brush the ribs with the BBQ sauce. Then let the ribs rest for 2 to 3 minutes.

Serve with more Oklahoma Joe's™ BBQ Sauce for dipping. Adding Sweet and Spicy Shoestring Potatoes (p. 113) to this dish will make a perfect match.

Remember never to fill your fryer more than half-full with oil.

Tips:

Unlike ribeyes or other steaks, beef ribs should be cooked until well done. The meatier end bones will take longer to cook than the less meaty middle bones. Don't be shy about cutting into them with a small sharp knife for a peek to see if they're done.

To please everyone at the table, you can serve the fried ribs with deep-fried ribeye steaks prepared in the same way. Cook 1-inch-thick ribeyes 2½ minutes for rare, 4½ minutes for medium rare, and 5½ minutes for medium. Remove them from the hot oil and let them stand at least 3 minutes.

When you add the ribs to the hot oil, the temperature will immediately drop. Don't worry, the ribs will cook fine at a slightly lower temperature. But if the temperature drops below 315° F., turn up the heat.

You must be very careful lowering the ribs into the hot oil. To be sure that the oil doesn't splatter, immerse the ribs 1 at a time and very slowly, using long handled tongs.

✳ ❀ ○ ❦

County-Fair Corn Dogs

Makes about 10

For a Kansas City–style variation, add some Oklahoma Joe's™ BBQ or Sweet & Spicy seasoning to the batter and serve with Oklahoma Joe's™ BBQ sauce for dipping.

The Batter
  1 cup all-purpose flour
  ⅔ cup stone-ground or regular cornmeal
  2 tablespoons sugar
  1½ teaspoons baking powder
  1 teaspoon dry mustard powder
  1 teaspoon salt
  1 large egg
  ¾ cup milk
  1 tablespoon vegetable oil

  1 pound hot dogs
  10 wooden popsicle sticks or 6-inch bamboo skewers
      Vegetable oil for deep frying

In a large bowl, combine flour, cornmeal, sugar, baking powder, mustard powder and salt. Whisk together well.

In a small bowl, whisk egg until slightly frothy; whisk in milk and oil. Add the mixture to the dry ingredients, stirring until just combined. Transfer the batter to a shallow dish.

Preheat the oil in a deep-fryer to 325° F.

Wipe hot dogs dry with a paper towel and insert a stick or skewer lengthwise into each. Roll four hot dogs in the batter (add a little additional milk to the batter if it doesn't coat well).

Add half of the corn dogs to the oil and fry until golden, turning occasionally with tongs (about 2 minutes). Transfer to paper towels to drain briefly. Repeat with the remaining corn dogs.

Serve with mustard, ketchup and relish.

Remember never to fill your fryer more than half-full with oil.

Coffee-Marinated Pork

6 servings

The Pork
½ cup cider vinegar
½ cup olive oil
¼ cup molasses
¼ cup chopped shallots
2 tablespoons finely ground espresso or other dark-roast ground coffee beans
1 tablespoon Dijon mustard
2 teaspoons ground black pepper
1 teaspoon salt
2 pork tenderloins (1 to 1¼ pounds each)
Vegetable oil for deep frying

The Salsa
1 cup diced fresh mango
½ cup slivered red onion
¼ cup chopped fresh cilantro or parsley
2 tablespoons olive oil
1 tablespoon fresh lime juice

1 small firm-ripe avocado
Salt to taste
Tabasco sauce to taste

PREPARE THE PORK

In a large dish, combine vinegar, oil, molasses, shallots, espresso, mustard, pepper and salt. Whisk to combine.

Fold over each tenderloin's narrow end and tie it in place with cotton kitchen twine to make the meat into a more even cylinder. Add to the marinade, turning to coat. Cover the dish tightly and refrigerate for at least 4 hours or overnight.

Heat the oil in a deep-fryer to 350° F. Remove the tenderloins from the marinade and pat dry with paper towels. Carefully add them one at a time to the oil and cook them until an instant-read thermometer inserted in the center registers 160° F. (10 to 12 minutes). Transfer the tenderloins to a cutting board and let them stand for 5 minutes to let the juices settle. Serve with the salsa.

PREPARE THE SALSA

Up to 2 hours ahead, combine salsa ingredients in a small bowl. Cover and refrigerate.

Just before serving, peel, pit and dice avocado and add it to the salsa. Season with salt and Tabasco to taste.

Remember never to fill your fryer more than half-full with oil.

Scotch Eggs

4 to 6 servings

Scotch eggs are hard-boiled, peeled eggs that are wrapped in a thin layer of bulk breakfast sausage meat, coated in breadcrumbs and deep fried. Children enjoy these treats as much as their parents do.

These tasty morsels can be served for breakfast or lunch, or as appetizers, and are extra good for taking on picnics and hunting trips, as they can be transported whole and then sliced into quarters for eating. Green salad and juicy tomatoes are a good accompaniment, as are pickled onions and mustard.

Scotch eggs are often served in pubs in the U.K., as they are great with beer.

6 eggs, at room temperature
1 tablespoon flour
1 pound bulk pork sausage
1 cup dried breadcrumbs
   Vegetable oil for deep frying

Place 5 of the eggs carefully in a bowl and cover them with warm water. Let them sit for 15 minutes, replacing the warm water as it cools. This will prevent the eggs from cracking when they are placed into boiling water.

Half-fill a saucepan with water, and bring it to a gentle boil. With a spoon, carefully lower the eggs, one at a time, into the boiling water, and turn down the heat to maintain a simmer. Cook for 11 minutes.

Pour off the boiling water and fill the saucepan with several changes of cold water. Immediately, tap each egg against the side of the pot to crack the shells, and then let them cool completely in the cold water. Peel off the shells, rinse the eggs and pat them dry.

Cut the sausage meat into 5 equal pieces. Pat each piece into an oval shape about ¼-inch thick. Hold one piece of the sausage in the palm of your hand and place an egg in the center; mold the sausage meat evenly around the egg to cover it completely, sealing any cracks. Repeat with the remaining eggs and sausage. Lightly dust the sausage-wrapped eggs with the flour.

In a shallow dish, beat the remaining egg, and spread half of the breadcrumbs on a sheet of waxed paper nearby.

Roll one of the sausage-wrapped eggs in the beaten egg until moistened all over, then roll it in the breadcrumbs until evenly coated. Transfer it to a tray. Repeat with the remaining sausage-wrapped eggs, using the other half of the breadcrumbs as needed.

Preheat the oil in a deep-fryer to 375° F. Fry the prepared eggs a few at a time until golden and crisp (4 minutes). Drain the eggs well on paper towels and let cool completely. Cut them lengthwise into quarters with a sharp knife, and serve them at room temperature.

The eggs can also be refrigerated whole for several days if desired—cold eggs are actually easier to cut than those at room temperature.

Remember never to fill your fryer more than half-full with oil.

Italian Stuffed Croquettes

Makes 18

An unusual and very tasty appetizer, these croquettes are crisp on the outside, and oozing on the inside. If you can get your hands on fresh mozzarella for this recipe, it will be well worth the investment.

2½ cups medium- or short-grain rice
6 tablespoons butter
1 cup grated Parmesan cheese
2 large eggs, beaten
Pepper, to taste
¼ pound prosciutto, in 18 thin slices
8 ounces mozzarella cheese, cut into 18 pieces
Fine, dry breadcrumbs, as needed
Vegetable oil for deep frying
Seasoned tomato sauce for dipping (optional)

Bring 5¼ cups salted water to a boil. Add the rice slowly, stirring. Cover and simmer slowly, until rice is tender, but still firm. Drain. Stir in butter until melted. Blend in Parmesan cheese, eggs and pepper. Cover and refrigerate until completely cool.

Divide the rice mixture into 18 parts. Take a portion of rice in your hand and press it flat with the back of a spoon. Set a piece of prosciutto in the center of the rice, and top with a piece of mozzarella. Close your hand to encase the prosciutto and cheese within the rice, then shape and smooth the croquette into a ball.

Repeat with all the rice, prosciutto and cheese. Roll the croquettes in breadcrumbs.

Preheat the oil in a deep-fryer to 380° F.

Carefully add croquettes to the hot oil with a pair of tongs, in batches of 5 or 6, and fry until golden brown and crisp.

Tips:

The best rice (that is readily available) to use for these croquettes is Arborio, an Italian medium-grain rice. Other good choices are Vialone Nano and Carnaroli, but an American medium- or short-grain rice is fine, as well.

If you dampen your hands with cold water, these croquettes will be easier to form. As your hands become sticky, give them another quick rinse.

Using a fryer basket, drain and transfer to a paper-towel–lined tray. Serve hot with tomato sauce, if desired.

Remember never to fill your fryer more than half-full with oil.

Potato-Crusted Beef Tenderloin

4 servings

Down-home cooking is often built around those old staples from the days of yore—meat and potatoes. With this quick, easy deep-frying recipe, you can now get both items in one delicious package.

Combine this dish with an appetizer of Fried Green Tomatoes (p. 25), a sidedish of Spicy Corn Fritters (p. 110) and Fried Ice Cream (p. 156) for dessert to make the all-American deep-fried meal!

PREPARE THE BATTER

Using a wooden spoon, in a medium bowl mix together the egg, milk, mustard, pepper, salt and butter until well combined. Stir in the potato flakes until the mixture has a uniform consistency.

Reminder: Always prepare your ingredients, utensils and working area before starting to cook. Frying demands your whole attention.

PREPARE THE MEAT

Working with one fillet at a time, coat each lightly in flour, knocking off any excess.

The Batter

- 1 egg
- 1 cup milk
- 1 teaspoon dry mustard
- ½ teaspoon freshly ground black pepper
- 2 teaspoons salt
- 3 teaspoons melted butter
- ½ cup instant mashed potatoes

The Meat

- 4 5-ounce medallions of beef tenderloin fillet
- ¼ cup flour
- ¾ cup large bread crumbs Vegetable shortening for deep frying

Cover each fillet in the potato mixture, then pat with the bread-crumbs. Set on a plate.

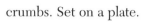

Arrange a paper-towel–lined sheet pan next to the fryer for draining the meat after it has been deep-fried.

Heat the shortening in a deep-fryer to 400° F. Carefully place the fillets in the hot oil and fry until crust is lightly golden (about 3 minutes). Serve hot with Dijon mustard.

Beef Empanadas

Makes about 12

Smaller versions of these Mexican turnovers make yummy hors d'oeuvres. Divide the dough into about 30 pieces, and fill and fry as directed.

The Filling
- 1 tablespoon vegetable oil
- 1 cup chopped onion
- 2 cloves garlic, minced
- 1 pound ground beef
- 1 tablespoon seeded and minced jalapeños
- 1 tablespoon mild chili powder
- 2 teaspoons ground cumin
- 1½ teaspoons dried oregano, crumbled
- 1 teaspoon salt
- 1 15-ounce can recipe-ready tomatoes
- 2 tablespoons tomato paste
- ½ cup pitted and chopped green olives

PREPARE THE FILLING

Heat oil in a large skillet over medium heat. Add onion and garlic and cook, stirring, until the onion is softened and beginning to color (about 3 minutes).

Add ground beef and cook, breaking it up with a wooden spoon, until no longer pink. Add jalapeños, chili powder, cumin, oregano and salt and cook for 1 minute longer.

Stir in tomatoes with their juice, tomato paste and olives. Adjust the heat to maintain a gentle simmer, and cook until the mixture has thickened and most of the liquid has evaporated (about 5 minutes). Set aside to cool completely.

PREPARE THE DOUGH

In a food processor, combine flour, baking powder and salt; pulse to combine. Add shortening and pulse until the mixture resembles coarse meal.

While the machine is running, slowly add the water; process until the mixture forms a ball of dough that

The Dough
  3 cups all-purpose white flour
1½ teaspoons baking powder
  1 teaspoon salt
  ½ cup vegetable shortening
  ⅔ cup water

    Vegetable oil for deep frying

is soft but not sticky; add more water or flour if needed. Cover the dough with plastic wrap and let rest for 30 minutes.

SHAPE THE EMPANADAS

Divide the dough into 12 equal pieces and roll each piece into a ball. On a lightly floured work surface, roll each ball out into a 6-inch circle. Stack the circles as you make them.

Put about ¼ cup of filling in the center of one of the circles. Generously moisten half of the circle edge with water and fold the circle in half, over the filling, pressing the edges firmly together. Trim off any ragged pieces with a paring knife and crimp the edge decoratively with the tines of a fork. Repeat with the remaining circles and filling.

Preheat the oil in a deep-fryer to 350° F. Add about 3 empanadas to the oil at a time and cook, turning once with tongs, until golden (about 2 minutes). Transfer to paper towels to drain briefly. Repeat with remaining empanadas. Serve hot.

Remember never to fill your fryer more than half-full with oil.

Pork and Cabbage Egg Rolls

Makes about 18

Serve these crispy Asian treats with small bowls of sweet-and-sour sauce and additional soy sauce for dipping.

The Filling
- 1 pound ground pork
- 3 cups mung bean sprouts
- 1 cup sliced green onions
  (2 bunches)
- 2 tablespoons vegetable oil
- 1 tablespoon minced fresh ginger
- 1 tablespoon minced garlic
- 1½ cups shredded carrots
- 1½ cups shredded cabbage
- 2 tablespoons rice wine vinegar
- 3 tablespoons soy sauce
- 1 tablespoon dark sesame oil
- 1 tablespoon cornstarch
- 1 pound egg roll wrappers
  (about 20)

PREPARE THE FILLING

In a large skillet, cook pork over medium-high heat, breaking it up with a wooden spoon, until no traces of pink remain. Add sprouts and green onions and cook, occasionally stirring, until the vegetables are wilted (about 2 minutes). Transfer to a bowl and set aside.

Add oil to the skillet; when it is hot—while constantly stirring—add garlic and ginger and cook until fragrant (about 10 seconds). Keep stirring and add carrots and cabbage. Cook for 1 minute.

Add vinegar and continue cooking the vegetables until they are tender (about 2 minutes more). Add the reserved pork mixture back to the skillet.

In a small bowl, stir together soy sauce, sesame oil and cornstarch until completely blended; add this to the skillet and continue stirring and cooking until the filling is well blended and thickened. Let cool completely.

The Egg Rolls
1 egg yolk
3 tablespoons water
2 tablespoons all-purpose
   white flour

Vegetable oil for deep frying

PREPARE THE EGG ROLLS

In a small bowl, whisk together egg yolk, water and flour to make a smooth mixture; set aside.

Place an egg roll wrapper on a work surface with one corner facing you. Place 2 generous tablespoons of filling in the center. Fold in the two side corners of the wrapper over the filling to meet in the center. Fold the corner closest to you up and over the two corners and the filling. Generously coat the remaining edges of the egg roll skin with the yolk and flour mixture. Roll up, pressing the edges in place to seal. Set on a baking sheet and repeat with remaining wrappers and filling.

Preheat the oil in a deep-fryer to 350° F. Carefully add 4 egg rolls at a time to the oil, turning them with tongs, until golden on all sides (1 to 2 minutes). Transfer to paper towels to drain and repeat with the remaining egg rolls.

Remember never to fill your fryer more than half-full with oil.

Tacos

Makes 1 dozen

Tacos taste best made from fresh corn tortillas. It is fun for people to choose their own toppings—if you are expecting a crowd, it's a good idea to have set-ups at two ends of the table so people don't have to crowd around one set of fillings and toppings.

The Filling
1½ pounds lean ground beef
2 garlic cloves, minced
3 tablespoons chili powder
1¼ teaspoons salt

12 fresh corn tortillas
Vegetable oil for deep frying

The Toppings
1 pound tomatoes, chopped
1 Spanish onion or large red onion, chopped
1 head iceberg lettuce
¾ pound shredded Monterey Jack or Cheddar cheese
1 jar green salsa
1 jar red salsa
1 pint sour cream

In a large preheated skillet, crumble the beef and cook, without stirring, over high heat until it begins to brown around the edges (about 6 minutes). Sprinkle with the garlic, chili powder and salt; stir the meat and cook until browned all over (about 4 minutes). Pour off the fat and divide the meat between two serving bowls.

Spread a layer of newspapers on a tray underneath a taco rack not too far from the deep-fryer. Preheat the oil in the fryer to 375° F.

Place a tortilla in a pair of taco-frying tongs and carefully lower it into the hot fat. Fry until golden and crisp (about 15 seconds), remove with the tongs and set the taco on the rack to drain and firm up. Repeat with the remaining tortillas.

As soon as the first tortillas are cool enough to handle, remove them to make room on the rack for the next batch. Serve warm and add the fillings of your choice.

Remember never to fill your fryer more than half-full with oil.

Down-Home Pork Chops and Applesauce

4 servings

This dish is always a crowd-pleaser when you have hungry folks at your table. Double the recipe as needed if you have more than 4 mouths to feed.

4 2-inch-thick, bone-in pork chops, 1 pound each
¾ cup all-purpose flour
1 egg
1 cup milk
1½ cups cornmeal
Vegetable shortening for deep frying
2 cups applesauce

Working with one chop at a time, toss it in flour, shaking off any excess. Coat each chop in egg, allowing excess liquid to drip off, and then pat with breadcrumbs. Place on a sheet pan. Repeat the coating process with each chop.

Preheat the shortening in a deep-fryer to 400° F.

Carefully place the chops in the hot oil with a pair of tongs. Fry them until the internal temperature registers 135° F. on an instant-read thermometer (typically about 7 minutes). Remove with the tongs to a paper-towel–lined sheet pan for draining.

Serve the pork chops with the applesauce and Potato Chips (p. 111).

Remember never to fill your fryer more than half-full with oil.

Seafood

Maryland Fried Rockfish

6 servings

Although we often think of blackening as the most appropriate way to cook white-fish such as rockfish, catfish and redfish, there are actually many ways to prepare these versatile fish.

Firm flesh and subtle taste make it a wonderful fryer, ideal for an all-you-can-eat fish fry. Don't forget the cole slaw and Hush Puppies (p. 11).

The Rockfish
    White cornmeal, as needed
    Salt and freshly ground
    pepper, to taste
1 tablespoon chili powder
1 teaspoon minced fresh thyme
1 teaspoon minced fresh oregano
2 pounds rockfish fillets
    Vegetable oil for deep frying
    Lemon wedges

PREPARE THE DIJON TARTAR SAUCE

Finely mince the parsley and the capers; place them in a medium bowl.

Add mayonnaise, mustard and lemon juice to the parsley and capers, blending well. Season to taste with pepper. Cover and refrigerate until needed.

PREPARE THE ROCKFISH

In a shallow dish, stir together cornmeal, salt, pepper, chili powder, thyme and oregano.

Preheat the oil in a deep-fryer to 375° F.

Dip both sides of the fish with cornmeal, patting off the excess. Place the fillets into a frying basket and carefully lower into the hot oil. Fry until nicely browned and crisp.

Tips:

Fish fillets fry very quickly, so watch them closely. Once the coating browns, your fish is most likely done as well. Remove it immediately while it is still juicy inside.

Dijon Tartar Sauce
- ¼ cup parsley leaves
- 1 tablespoon capers
- 1 cup mayonnaise
- 2 teaspoons Dijon mustard
- 2 teaspoons lemon juice
- Freshly ground pepper, to taste

Mix together all the tartar-sauce ingredients in a bowl. Transfer to a serving dish.

With the fryer basket, carefully lift the rockfish out of the hot oil, allow the excess oil to drain away and transfer the fillets onto a paper-towel–lined tray.

Serve hot with the Dijon tartar sauce and lemon wedges.

Remember never to fill your fryer more than half-full with oil.

Coconut Fried Shrimp

4 to 6 servings

These great hors d'oeuvres will make any party a hit. They are easy to make but will still impress your guests. The flaked coconut cooks up into a beautiful crisp-and-golden crust. If you can, use shrimp with the tails still on, and hold them out of the coconut when dipping. When you serve them, the tails will make great little handles for picking the shrimp off the platter.

1 cup flour
8 ounces light beer
1 teaspoon salt
1 pound large shrimp
2 cups shredded coconut
  Vegetable oil for deep frying

Stir together the flour, beer and salt in a large bowl.

Add the shrimp to the mixture, and stir to coat.

Spread the coconut in a shallow dish. One at a time, remove the shrimp from the batter and dredge them in the coconut.

Preheat the oil in a deep-fryer to 375° F.

Place a layer of shrimp in a fryer basket. Carefully lower into the hot oil, and fry until golden (about 1 minute). Remove the fryer basket, drain and transfer the shrimp to a paper-towel–lined tray. Repeat with remaining shrimp, and serve immediately.

Remember never to fill your fryer more than half-full with oil.

Clam Fritters

8 servings

For this dish, you can purchase frozen chopped raw clams from your fishmonger or at a quality supermarket; otherwise, you can use any fresh clams and chop them yourself. A 1-pound container of frozen chopped clams will yield the 1¼ cups you need for this recipe.

½ cup flour
½ teaspoon salt
⅛ teaspoon baking powder
⅓ cup milk
1 egg
1¼ cups chopped clams

Combine the flour, salt and baking powder in a medium bowl. Slowly whisk in milk until smooth, and beat in egg. Add the clams and mix well.

Preheat the oil in a deep-fryer to 375° F.

Carefully drop the fritter batter by heaping teaspoonfuls into the hot oil. Fry until golden (about 4 minutes). Remove with a slotted spoon, drain and transfer the fritters to paper towels.

Repeat with the remaining batter. Serve with lemon wedges, Down-Home Tartar Sauce (p. 91) or Dijon Tartar Sauce (p. 87).

Remember never to fill your fryer more than half-full with oil.

Chesapeake Crab Patties

4 to 6 servings

It is tastier by far to use fresh lump crabmeat in this recipe; however, the canned version is quite good, too.

If you prefer, make these into 12 very small patties and serve them as appetizers; note that the smaller pieces will cook faster.

These patties are extra good with your own easy-to-make tartar sauce.

The Patties
2½ cups crabmeat, picked over
　　 for shells
½ cup breadcrumbs
¼ cup chopped parsley
2 minced scallions
1 tablespoon Worcestershire
　 sauce
¼ teaspoon hot pepper sauce
2 eggs
¼ cup mayonnaise
½ cup all-purpose flour

In a large bowl, using a fork, lightly stir together the crabmeat, breadcrumbs, parsley, scallions, Worcestershire sauce, hot pepper sauce, eggs and mayonnaise.

On a lightly floured surface, shape the crab mixture into 8 small, or 6 larger, patties, turning to coat lightly with the flour.

PREPARE THE BREADING

Beat the egg and milk in a shallow bowl and spread the breadcrumbs on a sheet of waxed paper.

One at a time, dip the crab patties into the egg and then into the breadcrumbs. Let the patties sit while you heat the oil and set out a tray lined with paper towels for draining.

The Breading
1 egg
½ cup milk
¾ cup breadcrumbs
   Vegetable oil for deep frying

   Lime wedges
   Hot pepper sauce
   Tartar Sauce (home-made or
   store-bought)

Home-Made Tartar Sauce
1 cup mayonnaise
3 tablespoons fresh lemon juice
2 minced scallions
2 tablespoons chopped sweet
   pickle
2 tablespoons chopped parsley
1 tablespoon chopped capers

*Mix together all the tartar-sauce
ingredients in a bowl. Transfer to a
serving dish.*

Preheat the oil in a deep-fryer to 365° F.

Carefully slide half of the patties into the hot oil with a skimmer, and fry until golden brown (2 to 3 minutes).

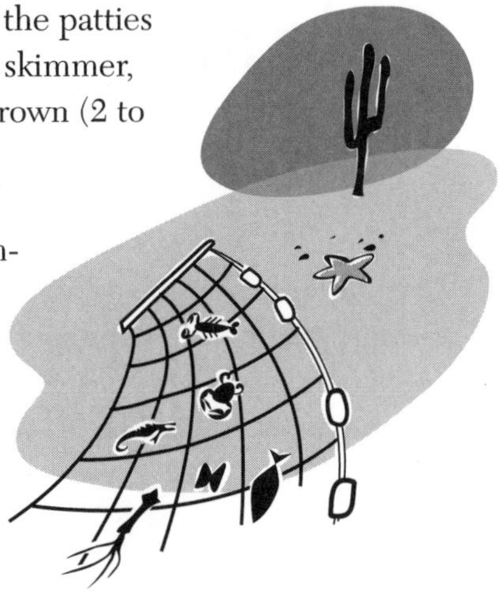

Remove with the skimmer and drain well on paper towels. Repeat with the remaining patties.

Serve hot and pass the lime wedges, hot pepper sauce and tartar sauce.

Remember never to fill your fryer more than half-full with oil.

Calamari

4 to 6 servings

Crisp little rings of deep-fried calamari, or squid, are often served in homey Italian restaurants. Sometimes they are simply dipped in seasoned flour before frying. This recipe calls for a batter with no eggs. The less squid are cooked, the more tender they will be, so cook them fast, in small batches.

1 cup all-purpose flour
½ cup cornstarch
1 teaspoon salt
1⅓ cups cold water
2 tablespoons fresh lemon juice
2 pounds small squid, pre-cleaned
Lemon wedges
Vegetable oil for deep frying

In a large bowl, mix together the flour, cornstarch and salt. Pour the water into the bowl and beat the mixture with a wire whisk until smooth. Stir in the lemon juice. Cover the batter and let it rest for about 1 hour.

With a sharp knife, cut the squid into rings, about ¼-inch thick. Cut the bunches of tentacles into bite-size pieces.

Spread layers of paper towels on a large tray for draining the fried pieces.

Preheat the oil in a deep-fryer to 365° F.

Dip several pieces of squid into the batter and drop them carefully into the hot oil. Cook until the batter is dry and lightly colored (1 to 2 minutes). With a skimmer, transfer the squid to the paper towels to drain. Repeat with more batches of squid. Serve while still warm, with lemon wedges.

Remember never to fill your fryer more than half-full with oil.

Conch Fritters

6 servings

1 pound conch, diced
1 clove garlic, minced
1 jalapeño, minced
1 medium onion, diced
1 tablespoon chopped parsley
2 cups all-purpose flour
1 tablespoon baking powder
½ teaspoon salt
1 cup water
  Salt, to taste
2 egg whites
  Vegetable oil for deep frying

In a large bowl, stir together conch, garlic, jalapeño, onion and parsley. In another bowl, sift together flour, baking powder and salt. Stir in the water until smooth. Stir in the conch mixture. Beat egg whites to stiff peaks and fold into batter.

Preheat the oil in a deep-fryer to 350° F.

In small batches, carefully drop batter by table-spoonfuls into the hot oil and fry until puffed and golden. Drain on paper towels, sprinkle with salt to taste and serve hot with hot sauce.

Remember never to fill your fryer more than half-full with oil.

Tips:

Conch can be found frozen and precooked. If it is not in small pieces already, it needs to be diced, otherwise you may find it a bit tough.

If you are lucky enough to be able to buy conch fresh, poach it very briefly (just until opaque), then cool and dice. Overcooked conch is difficult to chew. If you find that your conch has already passed the tender stage of cooking, keep it in the poaching liquid at a slow simmer until it is very well done—the additional cooking will make it tender again.

Chip-Shop Fish

4 servings

In most parts of Britain, a reliable fish dinner can be bought at the local "chippy," a slang word for a fish-and-chip shop. Their chips are something like our French fries but thicker and a bit softer—the perfect partner for fried fish in its own crunchy batter. Any "Limey" will perk up at the mention of this delicious dish.

For the most authentic experience, malt vinegar and salt are always served for sprinkling on this meal.

The Crunchy Batter
  1 cup all-purpose flour
  ½ cup cornstarch
  1 teaspoon salt
  1 teaspoon baking soda
1½ cups ice-cold water

The Chips
  4 large all-purpose potatoes, peeled

PREPARE THE CRUNCHY BATTER

In a large bowl, combine the flour, cornstarch, salt and baking soda. Pour in all of the water and stir with a wire whisk until smoothly blended. Cover and refrigerate until cold (about 1 hour).

PREPARE THE CHIPS

Cut the potatoes into long strips, about ½-inch thick. Soak the potato strips in a bowl of cold water for about 20 minutes to rinse out some of the starch. Drain well and pat dry with a towel. This step is important to minimize the splattering as you fry.

Preheat the oil in a deep-fryer to 375° F. Place half of the potatoes in a strainer basket and slowly lower them into the hot oil, raising and lowering the basket a few times until the oil stops bubbling up in the pot. Cook until golden (15 to 20 minutes). Drain well—you can even shake the

The Fish
4 fillets, cod or halibut,
  6 to 8 ounces each
½ teaspoon salt
¼ teaspoon pepper
¼ cup all-purpose flour

Vegetable oil for deep frying
Malt vinegar
Salt

basket over a grassy area—and spread on a rack in a warm oven. Repeat the process with the remaining potatoes.

PREPARE THE FISH

On a sheet of waxed paper, season the fish with salt and pepper and coat lightly with the flour.

Stir the batter.

Reheat the oil to 375° F. With tongs, carefully dip the fish into the batter and let the excess batter drip off. Place 2 pieces of the fish into the hot oil and fry until golden brown (about 4 minutes).

Drain the fish on paper towels or a wire rack, and keep warm in a low-temperature oven. Repeat with the remaining fish.

Serve the fish and chips immediately, sprinkled with malt vinegar and salt.

Remember never to fill your fryer more than half-full with oil.

Soft-Shell Crab on a Bun

6 servings

Scrumptious is the best word to describe these sandwiches. All you need is a side dish of salad or coleslaw and maybe an ice-cold beer. The juicy crabs will splatter the hot oil at first, so use great caution when frying these yummy morsels: Cover your arms, keep your face away from the oil and wear mitts to protect your hands.

1½ cups cornstarch
6 large soft-shell crabs,
   cleaned and patted dry
6 split hamburger buns, toasted
   Home-made tartar sauce (p. 91)
   Lemon wedges
   Vegetable oil for deep frying

Preheat the oil in a deep-fryer to 375° F.

Coat the crabs in the cornstarch, shaking off the excess. Using tongs, carefully lower the crabs into the hot oil and cook, three at a time, until golden (about 3 minutes). Transfer to paper towels to drain well.

Serve the crab on the freshly toasted bun with a spoonful of home-made tartar sauce (p. 91) and a lemon wedge on the side.

Remember never to fill your fryer more than half-full with oil.

Popcorn Shrimp

8 servings

For great flavoring, Oklahoma Joe's™ has done most of the work with their Sweet & Spicy seasoning by combining many different spices into one jar.

1⅓ cups all-purpose flour
1 tablespoon Oklahoma Joe's™ Sweet & Spicy seasoning
2 jumbo eggs, lightly beaten
2 cups milk
2 pounds baby shrimp, peeled and patted dry
2 cups plain dried breadcrumbs
Vegetable oil for deep frying

In a large bowl, combine the flour and Oklahoma Joe's™ seasoning. Make a well in the middle and pour in the eggs. Gradually pour in the milk, whisking constantly to remove any lumps. Let the batter rest for 30 minutes.

Prepare a tray lined with paper towels for draining the shrimp.

Preheat the oil in a deep-fryer to 365° F.

Stir the shrimp into the batter and pour it all into a colander set over a bowl. Add the breadcrumbs to the shrimp and toss together.

Working in batches, carefully add about 1 cup of shrimp to the hot oil. Fry until golden and crisp (about 2 minutes) and transfer to paper towels with a slotted spoon. Skim the leftover floating batter bits from the oil and repeat with the remaining batches. Serve hot.

Remember never to fill your fryer more than half-full with oil.

Oklahoma Fried Oysters

4 servings

People who would never try a raw oyster can rarely resist these wonderful and tasty fried mouthfuls.

1 egg
¼ cup milk
1 cup flour
1 cup yellow cornmeal
1 teaspoon Oklahoma Joe's™ Sweet & Spicy seasoning
½ teaspoon salt
Dash of black pepper
¼ teaspoon cayenne pepper
24 shucked oysters, well-drained
Lemon wedges
Hot sauce
Dijon tartar sauce (p. 87)
Vegetable oil for deep frying

Preheat the oil in a deep-fryer to 365° F.

In a bowl, beat together the egg and milk.

Spread half of the flour on a plate.

In another bowl, toss the cornmeal with the remaining flour, Oklahoma Joe's™ seasoning, salt, black pepper and cayenne pepper.

One at a time, dredge the oysters in the plain flour, then into the egg and finally into the cornmeal mixture. Spread them on a rack as you finish coating each one. Make sure that the oil does not overheat while you are busy coating the oysters.

Fry the oysters in small batches—crowding the pot lowers the temperature of the oil, resulting in greasy food—until golden brown (about 1 minute). Drain well on paper towels. Serve with lemon wedges and hot sauce, to taste. Dijon tartar sauce (p. 87) works well, too.

Remember never to fill your fryer more than half-full with oil.

Corn-Crusted Catfish

4 servings

Most catfish is now raised on farms, processed in factories and whisked away in refrigerated trucks to markets all over the country. But that won't stand in the way of enjoying this down-home favorite.

2	pounds catfish filets, patted dry
1	cup cornmeal
1	teaspoon salt
1	teaspoon pepper
½	teaspoon onion powder
½	teaspoon garlic powder (optional)
	Home-made tartar sauce (p. 91)
	Vegetable oil for deep frying

Preheat the oil in a deep-fryer to 375° F.

In a plastic bag, toss together the cornmeal, salt, pepper, onion powder and optional garlic powder.

Add the filets to the bag one at a time and shake to coat well.

When all of the filets are coated, slip them into the hot oil without crowding the fryer. As soon as they are golden brown, transfer the filets to a layer of paper towels to drain. Serve hot with Hush Puppies (p. 11), home-made tartar sauce (p. 91) and lemon wedges.

Remember never to fill your fryer more than half-full with oil.

Salmon Croquettes

4 to 6 servings

This is a tasty version of classic salmon croquettes. You can make it with any left-over fish, it you like, or make this easy version with canned salmon for a simple dinner or appetizer.

The White Sauce
- 3 tablespoons butter
- 3 tablespoons flour
- ¾ cup milk
- ½ teaspoon salt

The Croquettes
- 1 15-ounce can red salmon
- 1½ cups breadcrumbs
- ¼ cup chopped red onion
- ¼ cup chopped Italian parsley
- 2 tablespoons lemon juice
- 1 teaspoon grated lemon zest
- ⅛ teaspoon ground black pepper

- 2 eggs
- Vegetable oil for deep frying

PREPARE THE WHITE SAUCE

In a small saucepan, melt butter over medium heat. Add flour and whisk until smooth; cook 2 minutes, stirring. Whisk in milk and salt, stirring constantly until mixture is very thick and smooth (about 5 minutes). Remove from heat and set aside.

PREPRARE THE CROQUETTES

In a large bowl, combine salmon, ½ cup of the breadcrumbs, the chopped red onion, chopped Italian parsley, lemon juice, lemon zest and ground black pepper. Stir in the white sauce.

Refrigerate the salmon mixture until stiff, at least one hour. Spread remaining 1 cup breadcrumbs in a shallow dish. Lightly beat the eggs in a small bowl.

Roll mixture into 12 balls, rolling in bread-crumbs. Dip the balls in egg and roll in the breadcrumbs again. Refrigerate the salmon

Tips:

Lemon zest is the outer yellow part of the lemon peel. You can remove it with a fine grater or a zester. Either way, just be sure that you don't use any of the lemon's white part—it is very bitter.

balls until you are ready to cook them.

Preheat the oil in a deep-fryer to 365° F.

Place half the salmon croquettes in a fryer basket. Carefully lower them into the hot oil and fry until golden (about 2 minutes). Remove the fryer basket, drain and transfer the croquettes to paper towels. Repeat with the remaining salmon balls. Serve immediately.

Remember never to fill your fryer more than half-full with oil.

Fritto Misto

8 servings

These delicate tidbits of seafood, vegetables and cheese get their crunchy exterior from a subtle batter-coating mixture. Deep frying for Fritto Misto is done very briefly, so the foods you fry must be quite small or already tender.

The Batter
- 2 cups all-purpose flour
- 1½ teaspoons salt
- 4 large eggs, separated
- 1 12-ounce beer, at room temperature
- 2 tablespoons butter, melted

PREPARE THE BATTER

Sift together the flour and salt. In another bowl, beat the egg yolks until light. Blend in the beer and then the dry ingredients. Stir in the melted butter. Cover and refrigerate for 1 hour. Beat the egg whites until stiff (but not dry). Fold into the batter until no streaks remain.

Spread paper towels on a tray for draining the deep-fried pieces.

Preheat the oil in a deep-fryer to 375° F.

Roll whatever you plan to fry in flour, patting off excess, and roll in batter to coat completely. It may be better to flour and batter the pieces in batches, rather than all at once, as the batter is prone to slip off if the pieces sit exposed too long before frying.

Carefully drop the battered pieces into the hot oil—for this recipe, be sure to wear elbow-length oven mitts to protect your hands. Or, you can use

Tips:

As you fry, skim out bits of batter that are free floating; otherwise, they will burn and affect the taste of the frying oil.

Fry the cheese last, so it will still be oozing when served.

Any combination of the following, about 8 pieces per person:
- Eggplant, cut into ½-inch-thick sticks
- Zucchini, cut into 1-inch-thick rounds
- Onion, cut into ¼-inch-thick rings
- Mushrooms, trimmed
- Asparagus, cut into 2-inch lengths
- Cauliflower, cut into small florets
- Artichoke hearts, patted dry
- Shrimp, peeled and de-veined, the tail shell left on
- Jumbo lump crabmeat
- Sea scallops, patted dry
- Oysters, shucked
- Lobster tails, meat cut into chunks
- Gruyère cheese, cut into 1-inch chunks
- Fontina cheese, cut into 1-inch chunks

Vegetable oil for deep frying
All-purpose flour

a slotted spoon, immersing the bowl of the spoon in the oil, which allows the battered food to slip gently into the hot oil as opposed to splattering. Fry in small batches until golden brown (about 3 minutes).

Using a fryer basket, carefully drain and transfer the pieces to paper towels. Serve hot.

Remember never to fill your fryer more than half-full with oil.

Cornflake-Fried Oyster Po' Boys

Makes 4 sandwiches

Po' Boys are rumored to have begun life as a hand-out food from a certain coffee stand-café in New Orleans to "poor boys" who were union street-car workers on strike and standing in picket lines. Other regional names for this popular sandwich include heroes, grinders, subs and the pride of Philadephia, the hoagie.

4 6-inch-long soft French or
  Italian rolls
  Dijon Tartar Sauce (p. 87)
2 beefsteak tomatoes, sliced
  ¼-inch thick
1 cup thinly sliced iceberg lettuce

1 cup all-purpose flour
½ teaspoon salt
¼ teaspoon pepper
1 egg
2 cups Cornflakes,
  coarsely crushed
2 dozen freshly shucked oysters
  Vegetable shortening for
  deep frying

PREPARE THE OYSTERS

Lightly beat egg in a small bowl and set aside.

Mix together the flour, salt and pepper. Place flour mixture and Cornflakes in separate bowls or plastic bags.

Preheat the shortening in a deep-fryer to 350° F.

Pat oysters with a paper towel to remove excess moisture. Working with two at a time, toss oysters in flour mixture to coat, shaking off excess, then dip in egg. Roll the oysters in the Cornflakes (or shake in the plastic bag) to fully coat. Set the oysters aside on a paper-towel–lined sheet pan.

Working in batches of 6, fry oysters until golden brown (about 3 minutes each). Remove to drain on a paper-towel–lined sheet pan.

PREPARE THE PO' BOYS

Slice each roll in half lengthwise. Spread the Dijon Tartar Sauce (p. 87) on the rolls and top with tomatoes and lettuce. Place 6 oysters down the length of the roll.

Serve, and enjoy!

Remember never to fill your fryer more than half-full with oil.

Vegetables

Bright-Green Parsley Garnish

Servings vary with size of herb bunches

This is really a recipe for several kinds of fried fresh herbs, such as mint, sage or chives. They keep their bright color when fried and make a great garnish for all kinds of meat, fish and poultry dishes. Make sure that your herbs are absolutely dry before frying. Swish the herbs in a bowl of cold water and shake them thoroughly. Spread the herbs between paper towels and pat dry. It is possible to roll washed herbs loosely in paper towels and keep them in a refrigerator drawer for several days in preparation.

1 bunch Italian or flat-leaf parsley, washed and very dry
Vegetable oil for deep frying

Trim the long, tough stalks from the herb.

Spread paper towels on a tray for draining the fried parsley.

Preheat the oil in a deep-fryer to 365° F.

Being very careful of splatters, put a handful of the sprigs at a time into the oil and fry for about 30 seconds. With a skimmer or slotted spoon, transfer the parsley to the paper towels.

Remember never to fill your fryer more than half-full with oil.

French Fries

4 servings

The secret to fries is to use baking potatoes and to fry them twice. The first frying can be done several hours in advance, but the second frying needs to take place when you are ready to eat.

4 large baking potatoes
Vegetable oil for deep frying
Salt
Ketchup

Peel the potatoes, place in a bowl and cover with cold, salted water for 5 minutes to prevent discoloring. On a cutting board, carefully cut the potato into ¼-inch slices. Cut the slices into ¼-inch-wide strips, about 2½-inches long. Place the strips in cold water and let soak for about an hour.

Preheat the oil in a deep-fryer to 350° F.

Drain the potatoes well and pat the strips dry. Carefully add a handful of the strips to the oil, which will bubble up initially. Fry for 2 minutes, then remove with a wire skimmer and drain on paper towels. Repeat with the remaining batches. Let the fries cool completely before proceeding. Turn off the fryer until you are ready to serve the fries.

Heat the oil to 375° F. Fry the potatoes a second time until golden and crisp (2 to 3 minutes). Drain well on paper towels and serve at once with salt and ketchup.

Remember never to fill your fryer more than half-full with oil.

Spicy Corn Fritters

4 servings

Corn fritters can be sturdy or light. The beaten egg whites put these fritters into the light category. When separating the egg whites from the yolks, take care to see that no specks of yolk or grease gets into the whites, or they will not whip properly.

5 ears sweet corn, kernels scraped from the cob
2 jumbo eggs, separated
3 tablespoons all-purpose flour
1 teaspoon sugar
1 teaspoon Oklahoma Joe's™ Sweet & Spicy seasoning
¾ teaspoon salt
Dash of pepper
Vegetable oil for deep frying

Prepare a tray lined with paper towels to drain the fritters.

In a large bowl, combine the corn, egg yolks, flour, sugar, seasoning, salt and pepper. Stir to mix well.

Preheat the oil in a deep-fryer to 365° F.

In a clean, dry bowl, beat the egg whites with a whisk or electric hand-beater until they will hold soft peaks when flicked up. With a rubber spatula, fold the egg whites into the corn mixture.

Drop the mixture by rounded tablespoons into the hot oil. Do not crowd the pan, as they will cook quickly. Fry until golden (about 3 minutes). Use a slotted spoon or skimmer to drain and transfer them to paper towels. Serve hot.

Remember never to fill your fryer more than half-full with oil.

Potato Chips

4 servings

Chips can be addictive! It's a good idea to cook up a few batches, as they keep well for several days when cooled completely and stored in an airtight container.

Soaking the potato slices several times, which washes out the starch, may seem fussy, but it makes the chips really crisp. Patting them dry before frying is also key.

3 large baking potatoes
Vegetable oil for deep frying
Salt

Peel the potatoes and slice them paper thin; to make the job easier, use a vegetable slicer to cut even slices.

Soak the slices in a large bowl of cold water for 2 hours, changing the water at least 3 times during this length of time. Drain well and spread the slices in a single layer between paper towels and pat dry.

Preheat the oil in a deep-fryer to 375° F. Working in batches, drop about one-quarter of the chips into a strainer basket. Lower the basket into the hot oil, carefully raising it once or twice when the fat bubbles up. Cook, stirring if some of the slices stick together, until golden (2 to 3 minutes). The fewer chips in the fryer, the faster they cook. Drain well. Serve warm or at room temperature, sprinkled with salt.

Remember never to fill your fryer more than half-full with oil.

Broccoli in Breadcrumbs

4 to 6 servings

You can substitute cauliflower for broccoli if you like, in which case there will be no stems to peel. Serve as a side dish or as an appetizer.

1 bunch fresh broccoli
1 cup breadcrumbs
½ cup grated Parmesan or Romano cheese
½ teaspoon pepper
2 eggs
¼ cup milk
Vegetable oil for deep frying
Grated Parmesan or Romano cheese for sprinkling

Cut the stems from the broccoli, peel them and cut the stems crosswise into thin slices. Cut the broccoli head into bite-size florets.

On a plate, mix together the breadcrumbs, cheese and pepper.

In a bowl, beat the eggs and milk until blended.

Preheat the oil in a deep-fryer to 375° F. Dip each piece of stem into the egg mixture and then into the crumbs. With a skimmer or slotted spoon, transfer half of the stems to the hot oil. Fry until golden and drain on paper towels. Repeat with the remaining stems. Working in batches, coat and fry the florets. Sprinkle the broccoli lightly with cheese and serve at once.

Remember never to fill your fryer more than half-full with oil.

Sweet and Spicy Shoestring Potatoes

8 servings

The secret to these great fries is to make sure that you cut the potatoes thinly enough. You can use a handheld slicer, but it is also very easy to do with a knife. Use one that's very sharp, and take the time to do it well—the results of your labors will taste that much better!

2 pounds Idaho or russet potatoes
Vegetable oil for deep frying
Oklahoma Joe's™ Sweet & Spicy seasoning
Salt

Peel potatoes and place them in a bowl of cold water. Slice potatoes ⅛-inch thick. Stack the potato slices and slice the whole stacks lengthwise to make long, thin strips. As you cut the fries, put them back in the cold water.

Preheat the oil in a deep-fryer to 360° F.

One handful at a time, blot the potatoes dry and place them in a fryer basket. Carefully lower them into the hot oil and fry until golden (about 2 minutes). Remove the fryer basket, drain and transfer the potatoes to paper towels.

Sprinkle with Oklahoma Joe's™ Sweet & Spicy seasoning and salt. Repeat with the remaining potatoes. Serve hot.

Remember never to fill your fryer more than half-full with oil.

Plantain Crisps

8 servings

Plantains may look like bananas and are related to them, but as they are much more starchy, plantains are never eaten raw. When green, they are cooked in ways similar to those used for potatoes, but as they ripen and become sweeter, plantains are treated more like bananas—although always cooked before eating.

4 green plantains
2 tablespoons salt
Vegetable oil for deep frying

Cut the plantains crosswise into 3-inch sections, slit the skin lengthwise with a small, sharp knife and peel the skin off. Cut the plantains into 1-inch slices. Put the slices into a large bowl, sprinkle with salt and cover with water. Let sit 1 hour. Drain and pat plantains dry.

Preheat the oil in a deep-fryer to 375° F.

Fry plantains in a fryer basket in small batches until golden brown. Using the fryer basket, carefully drain and transfer to paper towels, and cool.

On a large piece of plastic wrap, place plantains and cover with another piece of wrap. Squash plantains flat with a meat mallet or rolling pin, but do not break them. (They should be about ⅛-inch thick.)

Repeating the process, fry a second time in small batches until golden brown on both sides. Drain as before, and serve hot.

Remember never to fill your fryer more than half-full with oil.

Zucchini Fritters

4 servings

Serve these as a sidedish or make
smaller ones and serve as appetizers.

1 pound small zucchini
Salt
2 scallions, minced
¼ cup chopped fresh parsley
1 teaspoon Oklahoma Joe's™
 Sweet & Spicy seasoning
½ teaspoon oregano
Dash of pepper
2 eggs, lightly beaten
½ cup all-purpose flour
Vegetable oil for deep frying
Lemon wedges
Hot sauce (optional)

Grate the zucchini coarsely, place it in a colander,
sprinkle with ½ teaspoon salt and let sit for 15 minutes over a bowl to drain.

Preheat the oil in a deep-fryer to 365° F.

In a medium bowl, combine the scallions, parsley,
Oklahoma Joe's™ seasoning, oregano and pepper.

Using a fork, stir in the drained zucchini. Stir in the
eggs and then the flour.

Working in batches, spoon rounded tablespoons of
the mixture into the hot oil and fry, turning once,
until golden (1 to 2 minutes). Drain well on paper
towels. Repeat with the remaining mixture. Serve
hot with lemon wedges and hot sauce, if desired.

Remember never to fill your fryer more than half-full with oil.

Potato Pillows

4 servings

These little treats will puff up into pillows as they fry. They cook quickly; as soon as they turn golden brown, they are done.

1 pound all-purpose potatoes, peeled and halved
½ teaspoon salt
½ cup all-purpose flour
¼ cup grated Parmesan cheese
Dash of pepper
Vegetable oil for deep frying

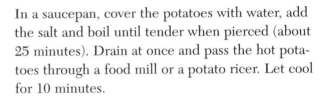

In a saucepan, cover the potatoes with water, add the salt and boil until tender when pierced (about 25 minutes). Drain at once and pass the hot potatoes through a food mill or a potato ricer. Let cool for 10 minutes.

With a fork, stir the flour, cheese and pepper into the potatoes.

On a lightly floured surface, roll out the dough to ¼-inch thickness and cut into rounds with a 2- to 3-inch floured biscuit cutter. Repeat, using the scraps.

Preheat the oil in a deep-fryer to 350° F. Add one-quarter of the potatoes to the oil and cook until browned and plumped. Remove the pillows with a long-handled skimmer or a slotted spoon. Drain on paper towels and repeat with the remaining batches.

Remember never to fill your fryer more than half-full with oil.

Chili-Lime Yucca Chips

Makes about 8 cups

Yucca chips can also be served with salsa, as a change of pace from the everyday tortilla chip. Serve these with cold drinks or on the side of any Mexican or South American-style meals that need a crunchy accompaniment, with or without the chili and lime.

2 pounds fresh yucca
Salt, to taste
Chili powder, to taste
Lime wedges
Vegetable oil for deep frying

Preheat the oil in a deep-fryer to 375° F.

Cut yucca into 4-inch lengths. Using a paring knife, cut a slit in the skin on the slices lengthwise and peel away skin and underlayer. Use a food processor, sharp knife or vegetable peeler to cut yucca into ⅛-inch-thick slices.

Using a fryer basket, carefully fry yucca in batches until lightly browned.

Drain and transfer to paper towels, sprinkle with salt and chili powder and serve warm. Pass lime wedges to be squeezed over the chips.

Remember never to fill your fryer more than half-full with oil.

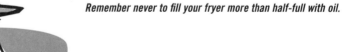

Succotash Fritters

12 servings

Look for fresh, shelled lima beans at farm stands and farmers' markets. They bear very little resemblance to canned limas that you may remember—and disdain— from childhood. In fact, fresh lima beans are one of summer's greatest vegetable pleasures. If you buy them in the pod, lima beans take a little time to prepare, but shelling beans provides a great opportunity to sit on the porch and shoot the breeze.

4 large eggs, separated
1 cup milk
2⅔ cups all-purpose flour
1 tablespoon baking powder
1½ teaspoons salt
   Freshly ground pepper, to taste
¼ cup minced chives
1 cup fresh corn kernels
½ cup diced red bell pepper
½ cup fresh lima beans (or frozen, and thawed)
   Vegetable oil for deep frying

Preheat the oil in a deep-fryer to 365° F.

In a large bowl, beat egg yolks until light. Blend in milk, flour, baking powder, salt and pepper. Stir in chives, corn, red pepper and lima beans. Beat egg whites to stiff peaks and fold in.

Carefully drop tablespoonfuls of the mixture into the hot oil and fry until light golden brown.

Remove with a skimmer, drain on paper towels and serve hot.

Remember never to fill your fryer more than half-full with oil.

Spicy Sweet Potato Fries

8 servings

These make a great pre-dinner appetizer that can be served out on the patio with some ice-cold beer or a pitcher of margaritas.

2 teaspoons salt
2 teaspoons Mexican-style (hot) chili powder
1 teaspoon dried oregano, crumbled
1 teaspoon ground cumin
4 large sweet potatoes (about 3 pounds total)
Vegetable oil for deep frying

In a small bowl, stir together salt, chili powder, oregano and cumin; set aside.

Peel sweet potatoes. Trim the ends of each potato, then stand on end and slice downward into ⅜-inch-thick slices. Stack several slices and cut into ⅜-inch sticks.

Preheat the oil in a deep-fryer to 350° F. Add half of the potatoes to the perforated strainer basket and carefully lower into the oil (the oil will bubble up). Cook until the fries are nicely golden (about 5 minutes), occasionally moving them around with tongs for even cooking.

With mitts, carefully lift the basket and fries out of the oil, and then transfer the fries to a brown paper bag. Sprinkle half of the reserved spice mixture over the fries and shake in the bag until evenly coated.

Repeat with the remaining potatoes. Serve hot.

Remember never to fill your fryer more than half-full with oil.

Sweet Potato Chips

Makes about 10 cups of chips

Chips can be made with a variety of root vegetables. While salt alone is always the perfect seasoning for a chip, it can be fun to sprinkle other things on them, too, such as cayenne (lightly!), ground sesame seeds, garlic salt or other seasoned salts.

2 pounds sweet potatoes
Salt, to taste
Vegetable oil for deep frying

Peel sweet potatoes. Use a food processor, sharp knife or vegetable peeler to slice sweet potatoes into ⅛-inch-thick rounds.

Lay the slices out on paper towels to dry for 10 minutes.

Preheat the oil in a deep-fryer to 375° F.

Using a fryer basket, fry the potato slices in batches until crisp and lightly browned. Drain and transfer to paper towels. Sprinkle with salt and serve.

Remember never to fill your fryer more than half-full with oil.

Carrot Fritters

2 dozen

Once you make the batter for this dish, you can set it in the refrigerator overnight for a nice deep chill.

½ cup flour
½ teaspoon salt
1 egg
1 tablespoon olive oil
½ cup beer
1 teaspoon curry powder
1 egg white, beaten to stiff peaks
¾ pound carrots, peeled and coarsely grated
Vegetable shortening for deep frying

Combine flour, salt, whole egg and olive oil in a large bowl until smooth. Slowly stir in the beer. Cover with plastic wrap and set aside at room temperature for at least 2 hours.

Preheat the shortening in a deep-fryer to 375° F.

Add the curry powder and mix until well combined. Gently fold in egg white, followed by carrots.

Carefully drop rounded tablespoonfuls of the mixture into the hot oil and cook for 1 minute per side. Using a slotted spoon, remove from oil to drain on a paper-towel–lined sheet pan.

Serve these delicious East Indian–style fritters warm.

Remember never to fill your fryer more than half-full with oil.

Green Tomato Puffs with Aioli

8 servings

There is nothing that says "summer garden" better than green tomatoes, a delicacy usually available only to home gardeners; however, the farmer's market will occasionally pick and sell a few early tomatoes. Later in the season, just before the first frost freezes the tomato crop, green tomatoes appear in piles at the farmstands. Use yours then, too, in this delicious preparation.

Aioli
- 4 cloves of garlic
- 2 large egg yolks
- 2 teaspoons Dijon mustard
- 1 tablespoon lemon juice
- ¼ cup extra-virgin olive oil
- ¾ cup vegetable oil
- Salt and freshly ground black pepper, to taste

PREPARE THE AIOLI

Mince the garlic and put it in a food processor or blender. Add egg yolks, mustard and lemon juice. Whirl until light in color. While the processor or blender is still on, very, very gradually pour in the oils. The aioli should thicken considerably. Season to taste with salt and pepper.

PREPARE THE TOMATOES

In a medium bowl, cover tomatoes with milk and set aside.

PREPARE THE BATTER

In a medium bowl, whisk together flour, baking powder, salt, parsley, thyme and cayenne. In another bowl, beat together egg yolks and buttermilk. Beat egg whites until stiff. Stir yolk mixture into dry ingredients. Fold in the egg whites.

Tips:

Aioli can also be made with the addition of smoothly pureed cooked potato, which gives the aioli a rustic richness. To adapt the recipe, simply whisk in about ½ cup of slightly warm, smooth potato puree. Adjust consistency with a bit of water if necessary, and add additional salt and pepper if needed.

The Tomatoes

- 6 medium green tomatoes, sliced into ½-inch-thick rounds
- 1 cup milk
- Vegetable oil for deep frying

The Batter

- 2 cups all-purpose flour
- 4 teaspoons baking powder
- 1 teaspoon salt
- 1 tablespoon chopped fresh parsley
- 1 tablespoon chopped fresh thyme
- Large pinch cayenne
- 4 large eggs, separated
- 1⅓ cups buttermilk

Preheat the oil in a deep-fryer to 375° F

Drain tomatoes one at a time and dip in batter, letting excess drip off. Fry in batches in a fryer basket until golden brown. Using the fryer basket, drain and transfer to paper towels. Serve hot, passing the aioli to dollop on top.

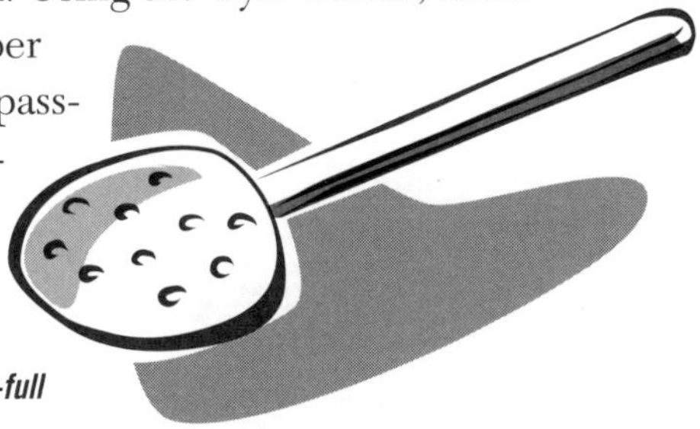

Remember never to fill your fryer more than half-full with oil.

Cajun Fried Okra

6 to 8 servings

2 pounds small, fresh okra
  Salt, to taste
3 cups yellow corn meal
½ teaspoon cayenne
½ teaspoon freshly ground pepper
  Vegetable oil for deep frying

Wash the okra in cold water and scrub lightly to remove any fuzz. Trim off stems. Bring a large pot of salted water to a boil. Add okra and cook 5 minutes. Drain and pat dry with paper towels.

Preheat the oil in a deep-fryer to 375° F.

Put cornmeal, cayenne and pepper into a brown paper bag and shake to mix. Add the okra and shake to coat it completely.

Fry the okra in batches until golden brown and crisp (about 2 minutes). Using fryer basket, drain and transfer to paper towels. Serve hot.

Remember never to fill your fryer more than half-full with oil.

Fried Plantain Cakes

6 servings

Plantain cakes are a wonderful accompaniment to a dinner of black beans and rice, with or without roast pork or chicken.

1½ pounds ripe plantains
1 tablespoon melted butter
1 tablespoon minced onion
1 tablespoon minced red bell pepper
1 tablespoon minced parsley
1½ teaspoons salt
Freshly ground pepper, to taste
1 large egg yolk
Vegetable oil for deep frying
Hot sauce

Preheat oven to 375° F. Cut ends off plantains and slit skin lengthwise. Set in a baking pan, slit-side-up, and bake until very tender (about 40 minutes). Cool.

Preheat the oil in a deep-fryer to 350° F.

Remove the plantains from their skins, mash them and put them in a bowl. Stir in butter, onion, bell pepper, parsley, salt, pepper and egg yolk. Form into 18 cakes.

Gently lower the cakes into the hot oil and fry until golden brown (about 2 minutes). Using the fryer basket, drain and transfer to paper towels. Serve hot, with hot sauce.

Remember never to fill your fryer more than half-full with oil.

Tips:

To be certain that your plantains are fully ripe, soft and sweet, buy them several days in advance, while still yellow, and let them sit at room temperature until completely black. Don't be put off by the color—inside, the flesh will be moist and yellow.

Beet Chips

Makes 13 cups

To slice beets thinly, you could use a very sharp knife and a steady hand, but it is easier with a slicing tool. You can buy a mandoline, a sturdy, metal professional tool. However, it is just as easy using a handy plastic slicer, sold in discount stores, on TV, or in Asian shops, where it is called a "Benriner."

2 pounds beets
Vegetable oil for deep frying
Salt

Peel or scrub beets under running cold water to remove any dirt or blemishes. Slice beets as thinly as possible.

Preheat the oil in a deep-fryer to 350° F. Place a large handful in fryer basket. Carefully lower into the oil and fry until golden (about 3 to 4 minutes). Remove fryer basket, drain and transfer beet chips to paper towels.

Repeat with remaining beet slices. Sprinkle with salt, and serve.

Remember never to fill your fryer more than half-full with oil.

Parsnip Ribbons

Makes about 4 cups

These long twists of fried parsnips are a fun, sweet addition to a basket of potato chips or beet chips. They can also be served alongside Oklahoma Joe's™ Sizzlin' Steak (p. 67) as an attractive accompaniment.

1 pound parsnips, peeled
Vegetable oil for deep frying
Salt to taste

Slice the parsnips into long ribbons with a vegetable peeler.

Preheat the oil in a deep-fryer to 350° F.

Place a layer of parsnips in a fryer basket. Carefully lower them into the hot oil and fry until just golden (about 1 minute). Remove the fryer basket, drain and transfer parsnip ribbons to paper towels.

Sprinkle with salt. Repeat with remaining parsnips. Serve warm.

Remember never to fill your fryer more than half-full with oil.

Deep-Fried Shallots

4 servings

This is a ridiculously easy topping for steaks, baked potatoes or mashed potatoes. This is one of the best kinds of recipes—in which very little effort can yield a delicious and versatile dish.

½ pound shallots
½ teaspoon salt
Vegetable shortening for
deep frying

With an extremely sharp knife, carefully cut the shallots into ⅛-inch-thin slices.

Preheat the shortening in a deep-fryer to 375° F.

Using a strainer basket, carefully lower all the slices into the hot oil, watching for splattering. Fry the slices until they are a deep, golden brown in color (about 4 minutes).

Remove to a paper-towel–lined tray, and spread over its companion dish just before serving.

Remember never to fill your fryer more than half-full with oil.

Deep-Fried Asparagus

4 servings

It is best to make this delicious dish in the springtime when asparagus is abundant and inexpensive, but you can make it whenever asparagus is available. Cooking time will depend upon the thickness of the asparagus spears.

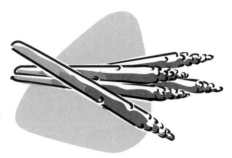

1 egg yolk
1 cup ice water
1¼ cups flour
1 pound asparagus
  Salt
  Lemon wedges
  Vegetable oil for deep frying

Whisk together the egg yolk and ice water. Slowly blend in the flour.

Preheat the oil in a deep-fryer to 375° F.

One at a time, dip the asparagus into the batter and carefully drop it into the hot oil. Fry until the asparagus spears are just cooked through (45 seconds to 2 minutes). Transfer asparagus to paper towels with a skimmer. Sprinkle with salt, and serve with lemon wedges.

Remember never to fill your fryer more than half-full with oil.

Falafel in Pita with Yogurt-Tahini Sauce

5 servings

These savory Middle Eastern spiced chickpea fritters have become commonplace in this country; the preparation usually starts with dried chickpeas that must be soaked and simmered, but this easier and faster version uses the canned variety, bound with some dry breadcrumbs.

The Yogurt-Tahini Sauce
1 cup plain yogurt
¼ cup chopped fresh cilantro or parsley
3 tablespoons tahini
1 tablespoon lemon juice
2 cloves garlic, minced
½ teaspoon salt
¼ teaspoon ground cumin

PREPARE THE SAUCE

Combine all ingredients in a bowl and whisk to combine; set aside.

PREPARE THE FALAFEL

In a food processor, combine chickpeas, breadcrumbs, egg, garlic, cumin, coriander, baking powder, salt and red pepper. Process until combined but still slightly grainy.

Shape the mixture into about 30 1¼-inch balls.

Heat the oil in a deep-fryer to 350° F. Line a baking sheet or platter with paper towels. Place half of the falafel in a perforated strainer basket and carefully lower them into the oil. Cook until crisp and deeply golden (about 2 minutes).

With mitts, lift the basket and falafel out of the oil;

The Falafel
  2 15-ounce cans chickpeas, thoroughly drained
  ¼ cup unseasoned dry breadcrumbs
  1 large egg
  3 cloves minced garlic
  2 teaspoons ground cumin
  1 teaspoon ground coriander
  1 teaspoon baking powder
  ¼ teaspoon salt
  ¼ teaspoon ground red pepper (cayenne)
     Vegetable oil for deep frying

  5 large pita breads with top third cut off
     Diced tomatoes
     Diced cucumber
     Chopped romaine lettuce

let drain briefly over the pot, then pour the falafel out onto the paper towels.

Repeat the frying process with remaining falafel.

For each serving, put about 6 falafel in a pita bread. Top with some chopped tomatoes, cucumber and lettuce, and drizzle with the yogurt-tahini sauce.

Remember never to fill your fryer more than half-full with oil.

Parmesan-Crusted Zucchini Sticks

4 servings

In August, this is a great way to use up all that extra zucchini in your garden!

2 pounds zucchini
2 eggs
¾ cup all-purpose flour
¾ cup finely grated fresh
   Parmesan cheese
½ teaspoon freshly ground
   black pepper
½ teaspoon salt
   Lemon wedges
3 sprigs parsley
   Vegetable shortening for
   deep frying

Cut the zucchini into sticks ½-inch thick by 3 inches long.

In a small shallow bowl, lightly beat the eggs. Set aside. In another bowl whisk together flour, Parmesan, pepper and salt, pour onto a plate and set aside.

Preheat the vegetable shortening in a deep-fryer to 375° F.

Coat the zucchini sticks in egg (letting excess drip off), then in Parmesan mixture (tapping to remove any excess). Set aside on a plate in a single layer, making sure the pieces are not sticking to each other.

Carefully fry in single-layer batches until golden (3 to 5 minutes). Be sure to allow the sticks enough room to fit without touching each other. Remove with a strainer basket to a paper-towel–lined sheet pan for draining, and sprinkle with additional salt, to taste. Serve with lemon wedges and parsley.

Remember never to fill your fryer more than half-full with oil.

Boilin'

Beer-Cooked Sausage BBQ Sandwiches

8 servings

These hearty sandwiches are perfect for a crowd of hungry beer lovers. Be sure to also serve a big pile of napkins and—of course—plenty of icy-cold beer!

¼ cup vegetable oil
4 large onions, sliced
2 12-ounce bottles of beer
½ cup Oklahoma Joe's™ BBQ sauce
½ teaspoon ground black pepper
¼ teaspoon salt
8 sausages, about 2½ pounds total
8 hard rolls

PREPARE THE SAUSAGES

Prick sausages all over, either with the tines of a fork or with the point of a sharp knife. This will keep them from bursting.

Heat the oil in a large pot over a medium heat. Add the onions and cook, stirring occasionally, until tender (10 to 15 minutes).

Stir in beer, Oklahoma Joe's™ BBQ Sauce, pepper and salt. Add sausages and bring to a boil. Reduce heat and simmer, turning the sausages and stirring occasionally, until sausages are cooked through (about 20 minutes).

Using tongs, remove sausages and set aside. With a slotted spoon, remove onions to a side bowl and set aside.

PREPARE THE SAUCE

Increase heat to high and boil the remaining liquid uncovered until it is fairly thick and saucy

Tips:

This recipe is best made with bratwurst, but you can prepare it with any variety of uncooked sausages. Italian sausages work very well. And if you like spice, use hot Italian sausages.

You can use any variety of beer for this recipe, but know this: the flavor of the beer will be intensified in the cooking. If you want a mild beer flavor, use a light lager. If you want a stronger flavor, use a dark ale. You should probably stay away from stouts and porters because the flavor will be too intense.

(about 10 minutes). Return the sausages and onions to pot just to heat through. Remove from heat.

MAKE THE SANDWICHES

Split the rolls lengthwise without cutting all the way through. Place one cooked sausage in each bun, top with BBQ onions and drizzle with sauce.

Take the beers out of the fridge or cooler and serve everything immediately!

Crawfish Boil

4 servings

Although this recipe serves 4, it seems only natural to invite a crowd for a crawfish boil. To increase the amounts, simply double or triple all ingredients. Be sure to let the cooking broth come back to a simmer once the crawfish have been added—it will take longer with more water and more crawfish—and then simmer for about 5 minutes.

The Cooking Broth
1 gallon water
2 bay leaves
4 large sprigs fresh thyme
1 onion, quartered
1 bottle dry white wine
½ to 1 teaspoon cayenne, depending on preferred hotness
½ teaspoon allspice
6 whole cloves

PREPARE THE BROTH

Put all ingredients for cooking broth into pot, bring to a simmer and cook for 20 minutes.

PREPARE THE CRAWFISH

Add crawfish and bring broth back to a simmer. Cook about 5 minutes, until the crawfish are bright red.

Pour crawfish and cooking liquid into a very large bowl and set aside to cool for 15 minutes. Drain and pile on a platter.

Serve with lemon wedges and hot sauce.

To peel the cooked crawfish, twist the tail off the body and peel it. The meat in the tail is just about all the eating there is on a crawfish, although some people like to "suck the heads" as well,

4 dozen fresh crawfish (thawed, if frozen)

Lemon wedges
Hot sauce

enjoying the juice found in there. You will also find a bit of edible and delicious fat between the tail and the body.

Chicken Gumbo

6 to 8 servings

Gumbo is a classic Creole dish and a great crowd-pleaser. This recipe can be doubled or even tripled, if you like.

1½ cups diced smoked bacon
¼ cup vegetable oil
2 onions, chopped
1 cup diced celery
1 cup diced green pepper
2 cloves garlic, minced
¼ cup flour
1 28-ounce can whole tomatoes in juice, cut up
1 14.5-ounce can chicken broth
2 teaspoons chopped fresh thyme leaves
½ to 1 teaspoon cayenne pepper
½ teaspoon salt
¼ teaspoon ground black pepper
12 skinless chicken thighs
2 cups corn
2 cups okra cut in ½-inch pieces
2 teaspoons file powder (if available)

Cook bacon in th oil over medium heat for 2 minutes. Add onion, celery, green pepper and garlic, and cook until tender (about 10 minutes). Stir in flour, then tomatoes, chicken broth, thyme, cayenne, salt and black pepper. Add chicken pieces.

Bring mixture just to boil, reduce heat and simmer until chicken is very tender (about 45 minutes). Add corn and okra, and simmer until okra is just tender (about 8 minutes).

Stir in file powder, and add salt and pepper to taste. Serve with rice.

Tips:

File powder, made from the dried leaves of the sassafras tree, is one of the classic gumbo ingredients. It slightly thickens the stew and gives it a distinctive flavor. Be sure that you don't cook it for too long or the gumbo will become too thick and gelatinous.

If fresh okra and corn is not available, you can use frozen. Go ahead and add it straight from the freezer. But if you use frozen, it barely needs to be cooked, so watch carefully so that the okra doesn't overcook.

You can make this gumbo recipe with shellfish if you prefer it to chicken. Simply simmer the mixture without the chicken and add shellfish such as crab or shrimp along with the corn and okra. Cook the mixture just until the shellfish and okra are cooked through.

If you like your gumbo super hot and spicy, add a bit more cayenne. If you are making it for a crowd, cook it up with less cayenne and serve it with a bottle of your favorite hot sauce for your guests to stir in and spice it up according to their tastes.

Brunswick Stew

8 servings

Traditionally, Brunswick Stew included rabbit, pork and sometimes squirrel and was typically eaten alongside barbecue. While this version is a lightened update—with chicken rather than an assortment of meats—it retains Brunswick Stew's original down-home heartiness, making it an ample main dish.

6 pounds chicken pieces
   All-purpose flour, seasoned
   with salt and pepper
6 tablespoons butter
1 large onion, chopped
1 28-ounce can tomatoes,
   chopped
1½ teaspoons dried thyme
2 cups fresh corn kernels (or
   thawed, if frozen)
2 cups fresh lima beans (or
   thawed, if frozen)
   Salt and freshly ground black
   pepper, to taste
¼ cup chopped fresh parsley

Dredge chicken in seasoned flour and pat off excess. Melt butter in a very large pot over medium-high heat and add the chicken; brown it on all sides. Remove chicken and set aside. Add onion and cook until well browned, stirring often, about 8 minutes. Replace chicken and add tomatoes and thyme. Add water to cover, if needed.

Cover and simmer until chicken is tender (20 to 30 minutes). Add corn and lima beans and simmer an additional 5 minutes. Season to taste with salt and pepper, stir in parsley and serve.

Louisiana Steamed Shrimp

8 servings

Everybody gets a kick out of peel-and-eat shrimp, and it is not often that you can get enough of these tasty delights. Four pounds of shrimp should be enough to satisfy eight hearty appetites and still leave a handful to eat cold the next day.

The Spice Mix
- 4 teaspoons chili powder
- 2 teaspoons cayenne
- 2 tablespoons paprika
- 2 teaspoons mustard powder
- 2 teaspoons dried oregano
- 2 teaspoons dried thyme
- 1 tablespoon salt
- 1 teaspoon pepper
- 4 bay leaves, crumbled

- 4 pounds large shrimp, unpeeled
- 2 quarts water

In a small bowl, stir together all the ingredients for the spice mix. Put the 2 quarts of water into the pot and bring to a boil. Add the shrimp, sprinkle with spice mix and stir gently. Cover and cook until the water returns to a boil. The shrimp should be fragrant, firm and opaque. If not, let them cook a little longer. Otherwise, remove to a large platter and serve hot. Be sure to provide lots of paper napkins and a bowl for shrimp shells.

Tips:

While you are making the spice mix, double or triple the recipe and set some aside for another time. Once the spice mix is made, there is nothing simpler than spiced shrimp.

Lobster Boil

4 servings

When you choose lobsters, go to reputable fishmongers—they typically have clean lobster tanks that are not overcrowded and clean stores that smell like the ocean (not like fish!). Lobsters should be very spry and active when you pull them from the tank. As lobsters are very perishable, they generally won't last more than a day in the refrigerator. A 1½ pound lobster serves 1 person.

4 1½ pound lobsters
2 sticks butter, melted
2 lemons, cut in half

Fill the pot ⅔ full of water. Bring to a rolling boil.

Place lobsters in the boiling water head-first and cover. Once the water has returned to a boil, cook for 10 minutes.

Remove the cooked lobsters with tongs, holding them by the tail to release water for the most efficient draining.

Serve each lobster with a small bowl of melted butter and a lemon half. Traditionally, lobsters are eaten by both adults and children with a lobster bib, lobster or seafood fork, and crackers. The bib protects you from the messy, watery process of taking a lobster apart. You may want to wrap the lemon halves in a layer of cheesecloth—this strains the pits from the juice.

This recipe matches up very well with Perfect Boiled Corn (p. 147) and Fried Ice Cream (p. 156).

Tips:

Lobsters go into a sleep-like state when they are cold. For a more humane cooking treatment, put them in the freezer for about 10 minutes before plunging them head-first into the boiling water—the easiest way to get them into the pot. Lobsters should always be alive just before you cook them.

To eat a lobster, remove the tail by twisting it off. You may find the tomalley (liver) here, or the red roe (eggs) if your lobster is female. (The eggs are an acquired taste!) Snip the tail shell with kitchen shears on the underside lengthwise from the widest part to the end of the tail. Open the shell like a book and remove the meat. Next remove the claws; don't forget the knuckle of the lobster—this has a large chunk of meat. Using lobster crackers, crack the shell and peel it away, revealing the meat. Dip the meat in melted butter or squeeze fresh lemon on it. The body of the lobster does not have that much meat in it, but you may remove the small legs on the underside of the body and squeeze the meat out of them with your teeth or your lobster fork.

Smoky Chili Con Carne

8 servings

Everybody loves chili. This tasty recipe uses smoked chipotle peppers that give this scrumptious dish an extra-special smoky flavor. Even though tried-and-true "chili heads" traditionally don't use beans or ground beef in their recipes, this contemporary classic is easy to make at home anytime. It's also perfect for a tailgate party!

¼ cup vegetable oil
2 cups chopped onion
2 minced garlic cloves
2 pounds ground beef
1 tablespoon chili powder
1½ teaspoons ground cumin
1 15-ounce can pinto beans
2 28-ounce cans crushed tomatoes in purée
4 chipotle peppers in adobo, chopped
½ teaspoon salt
½ teaspoon ground black pepper
Chopped white onion
Shredded Monterey Jack cheese
Sour cream

PREPARE THE CHILI

In a large pot, heat the oil over medium heat. Add onion and garlic and cook, stirring frequently, until onions are tender (about 10 minutes).

Add ground beef, chili powder, and cumin. Cook, breaking up the meat and stirring occasionally, until the meat is no longer pink (6 to 8 minutes).

Rinse and drain the pinto beans.

Add canned tomatoes, pinto beans, chopped chipotle peppers, salt and black pepper. Cook, stirring occasionally, until the mixure is thick and the flavors have blended (35 to 45 minutes).

Serve in bowls, topped with chopped onion, shredded Monterey Jack cheese and sour cream.

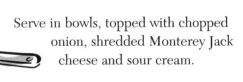

Tips:

You can substitute any variety of bean for this recipe, or if you don't like beans, leave them out. You can also use dried beans that you soak and cook yourself. Two cups of cooked beans is a perfect substitute for the canned beans.

Canned chipotle peppers in adobo are available in the Mexican section of the supermarket. If you cannot find them, you can use 2 dried chipotle chiles. Soak them in warm water to soften and then purée before adding.

Don't use very lean ground beef for this or any chili recipe. Using beef with at least 20% fat will give the chili much better flavor.

This recipe can be doubled, tripled or even quadrupled. If you do, each step of the recipe may take a few minutes longer, so don't follow the times in the recipe. Pay attention to the descriptions instead.

Mussels Meuniere

4 to 6 servings

This classic dish can be served either as an appetizer or a main course. Serve it with a loaf of crusty bread to soak up the tasty broth.

¼ cup olive oil
1 cup chopped shallots or yellow onion
4 minced garlic cloves
½ cup white wine
½ cup chopped Italian parsley
4 pounds mussels

CLEAN THE MUSSELS

Clean the mussels as well as possible, scrubbing with a scrub brush and scraping off any barnacles that are stuck to them. Discard any mussels with broken shells as well as any mussels that do not open and close again after you tap them lightly.

PREPARE THE MUSSELS

Heat the olive oil in a large pot. Add the shallots and garlic and cook, stirring, until tender (6 to 8 minutes). Stir in white wine and ¼ cup of the parsley. Cook until wine is slightly reduced and you no longer smell alcohol.

Add mussels to pot, cover and cook over high heat, stirring them occasionally, until all of the mussels open (8 to 10 minutes).

Scoop out mussels and place in serving dishes. Ladle the broth over the mussels and sprinkle with the remaining chopped parsley. Serve warm, and be sure to put out a plate for the discarded shells.

Perfect Boiled Corn

4 servings

There have always been debates over the best way to
cook corn. Some say you should boil it for 3 minutes,
others say 5 minutes, still others say only steam it, and
so on. But the truth is that today's super-sweet corn

doesn't really need to be cooked at all. The kernels are delicious raw and can be
cut straight from the cob to use in salads. The only real reason to cook it at all is to
heat it through so that the butter you put on it will melt! This method makes perfect hot corn on the cob every time.

4 to 16 ears of corn
water

Husk corn. Bring to boil enough water to cover the
corn. Add corn cobs, cover and remove pot from
heat. Wait 5 minutes and remove corn from water.
That's it.

Bollito Misto with Salsa Verde

12 servings

Somewhat similar to the French dish, Pot au Feu, Bollito Misto is a mixture of meats, vegetables and aromatics, simmered slowly to meld flavors and tenderize chicken, beef, sausage and veal. As a meal to be savored, it's a terrific choice for gatherings of family, extended family or friends.

1 3½-pound chicken, whole
1 pound beef rump
2 pounds cotechino sausage
2 tablespoons salt
2 bay leaves
1 1-pound veal tongue (optional)
12 carrots, peeled and halved
12 medium onions, peeled and quartered
12 medium potatoes, peeled

Put the chicken, beef rump, sausage, 1 carrot and 1 onion into a large pot and cover with cold water. Bring to a simmer, skim, and add salt and bay leaves. Simmer one hour.

Add the tongue and simmer 30 more minutes.

Add the remaining carrots, remaining onions, potatoes and enough cold water to cover. Increase heat to bring the pot back to a simmer. Reduce heat and simmer for 30 more minutes.

Turn heat off and let sit for 15 minutes.

PREPARE SALSA VERDE

Put all ingredients into food processor and pulse until finely minced, but not pureed.

To serve Bollito Misto, slice tongue, cut chicken into

Tips:

Cotechino sausage is an Italian fresh pork sausage. Look for it at your local Italian deli.

Serve Bollito Misto in large, shallow bowls so you will be able to ladle some tasty broth over each serving. Set small bowls for Salsa Verde to the side of each place-setting, so each bite may first be dipped.

Salsa Verde
  3 tablespoons red wine vinegar
  ½ cup olive oil
  2 anchovies
  1 tablespoon capers
  1 clove garlic, chopped
  ½ teaspoon Dijon mustard
  2 tablespoons chopped parsley

pieces and cut beef into manageable chunks.

Arrange on a large, deep serving platter, surround with vegetables and pour some hot broth over all.

Serve with Salsa Verde.

Shrimp and Corn Feast

8 servings

Although shrimp is available year-round, the best sweet corn is always in the late spring and summer. Make this dish for your hungry clan during the dog days, after the kids are home from their Little League game and it's still light out well into the evening hours. This is also a terrific cook-out dish for the beach.

The Seafood Dipping Sauce
- 2 red bell peppers
- 1 medium sweet onion
- 3 medium tomatoes
- ⅓ cup cider vinegar
- ⅓ cup brown sugar
- 1 teaspoon salt
- Pinch of ground cloves
- Pinch of celery seeds
- Pinch of dry mustard

PREPARE THE SEAFOOD DIPPING SAUCE

Chop the red peppers, the sweet onion and the tomatoes coarsely. Put them into a food processor and chop very thoroughly, but do not puree them. Transfer to a medium, non-reactive saucepan and stir in all remaining ingredients. Bring to a simmer and cook until thickened somewhat (about 30 minutes). Stir often and do not let the sauce burn on the bottom. Set aside to cool until needed.

PREPARE THE SHRIMP

While the sauce is cooking, set aside 1 tablespoon of the seafood seasoning. In a large pot, stir together remaining seafood seasoning, thyme, salt, water and beer. Bring to a boil.

In the meantime, cut the onions into wedges, cutting through the core to keep the wedges in one piece.

Add the potatoes and onions to the cooking liquid.

The Shrimp
½ cup seafood seasoning
1 teaspoon dried thyme
1 tablespoon salt
3 quarts water
2 12-ounce beers
4 medium sweet onions
16 small red potatoes
8 ears corn
4 pounds large shrimp in shells
2 tablespoons chopped
   fresh parsley

Melted butter
Lemon wedges

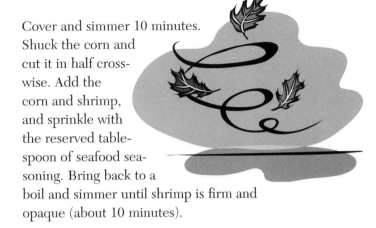

Cover and simmer 10 minutes. Shuck the corn and cut it in half crosswise. Add the corn and shrimp, and sprinkle with the reserved tablespoon of seafood seasoning. Bring back to a boil and simmer until shrimp is firm and opaque (about 10 minutes).

Arrange potatoes, onions, corn and shrimp on large platters. Sprinkle with chopped parsley. Serve with seafood dipping sauce, melted butter and lemon wedges on the side.

Be sure to provide a large bowl for shrimp shells and corn cobs, and put out lots of paper napkins!

Easy Bouillabaisse

6 servings

There are many varieties of Mediterranean fish stew. This is one of the simplest. It is perfect for a summer evening when tomatoes are in season.

¼ cup olive oil
2 cups chopped onion
2 cloves minced garlic
½ cup chopped Italian parsley
½ cup dry white wine
1 long strip orange peel
2 teaspoons chopped fresh tarragon leaves
2 pounds clams or mussels, scrubbed
1½ pounds firm fish fillets or steaks
3 cups ripe diced tomatoes
½ teaspoon salt
¼ teaspoon ground black pepper

French bread slices

Heat the olive oil over medium heat. Add the onion, garlic and ¼ cup of the chopped parsley. Cook until the onion is translucent.

Add wine, orange peel and 1 teaspoon of the chopped tarragon, and cook until slightly reduced. Add clams or mussels, cover and cook until they open (5 to 10 minutes). With a large slotted spoon, remove mussels or clams. Place in a bowl and set aside.

Cut the fish into 1-inch cubes.

Add tomatoes, salt and pepper to the onion mixture, and bring just to simmer. Add fish and cook, stirring occasionally, until fish is just cooked through (about 5 minutes).

Return clams or mussels to the pot. Stir gently.

Place a slice of French bread in the bottom of each serving bowl. Top with a ladleful of fish stew and sprinkle with the remaining ¼ cup chopped parsley and 1 teaspoon chopped tarragon. Serve immediately.

Tips:

You can make this easy fish stew with many different types of fish and shellfish. Just make sure that you use varieties that do not fall apart when you cook them. Some of the best are swordfish, grouper, monkfish and tuna. Ask your fishmonger which fish are freshest and then which of those will be best in a stew. Thin, flaky fish fillets, such as snapper and flounder, will fall apart.

Be sure that you use only ripe tomatoes for this stew, otherwise you will not have enough broth. If you prefer a soupier stew, you can add a small bottle of clam juice to the mixture along with the tomatoes.

To remove a strip of orange peel from an orange, use a vegetable peeler. You should use a navel orange and be sure that you clean it well before taking the peel.

New England Boiled Dinner

8 servings

The term "corned" in corned beef refers to the kernel-size salt crystals used to brine beef brisket and beef round. Salting was originally done to preserve meat before the days of refrigeration. These days we continue to enjoy corned beef for its unique flavor, achieved through a mixture of seasonings such as garlic, pepper and allspice, in addition to the salt.

6 pounds corned beef brisket
½ teaspoon freshly ground black pepper
2 bay leaves
8 large carrots, cut into chunks
8 medium all-purpose potatoes, peeled and halved
1 medium green cabbage
1 tablespoon chopped fresh parsley

Sauce
3 tablespoons horseradish
5 tablespoons sour cream

Put corned beef into pot and cover with water. Add pepper and bay leaves, and bring to a simmer. Simmer for 3 hours. Add carrots and potatoes. Simmer 40 more minutes. Cut cabbage into wedges, leaving the core in the center to hold wedges together. Add cabbage to pot and simmer 20 more minutes.

Meanwhile, make the sauce by stirring together horseradish and sour cream.

Remove beef, slice it and arrange it on a large platter. Surround with carrots, potatoes and cabbage. Sprinkle with parsley and serve immediately. Pass horseradish sauce separately.

Desserts

❄ ❋ ☼ 🍂

Fried Ice Cream

4 to 5 servings

Freeze the ice cream balls very hard and have all the serving utensils and dishes (and your guests!) ready before you start frying. The coated balls can be frozen in shallow containers for several days prior. You can serve them with a drizzle of store-bought fruit syrup, such as raspberry, strawberry or black currant. If you plan on doubling this recipe for a crowd, make the coating in separate batches, as it gets messy.

2 pints rich vanilla ice cream
1 extra large egg white
¼ teaspoon cinnamon
1¼ cups chopped nuts, such as almonds or peanuts
Vegetable oil for deep frying
Fruit syrup (optional)

Place a tray in the freezer until very cold. With an ice cream scoop, shape the ice cream into balls and drop them onto the cold tray. Quickly return them to the freezer until firm (about 1 hour).

Place the egg whites and cinnamon in a bowl and beat lightly until the whites are just frothy. Spread the nuts on waxed paper.

Working quickly, roll the ice cream in the egg white, then into the nuts. Roll once more in egg white and nuts and return them to the freezer. Freeze hard while you prepare the oil for frying.

Preheat the oil in a deep-fryer to 375° F. Transfer 4 of the balls from the freezer to the hot oil with a skimmer. Fry for 10 to 15 seconds, then transfer the balls to dishes and serve immediately, with syrup if desired. Repeat, until all of the balls are fried.

Remember never to fill your fryer more than half-full with oil.

Apple Fritters

4 to 6 servings

Apple fritters were popular many years ago. We think it's time they made a comeback.

For best results, use Golden Delicious apples, which are sweet, or Granny Smith apples, which are tart.

Dust the hot fritters generously with sugar, or drizzle them with maple syrup and some softly whipped cream for a special dessert treat.

2 large eggs
⅔ cup apple juice
1 tablespoon melted butter
1 cup all-purpose flour
½ teaspoon allspice or cinnamon
  Pinch of salt
4 Golden Delicious or Granny Smith apples
  Juice of half a lemon
  Confectioners' sugar for dusting
  Vegetable oil for deep frying

In a bowl, whisk together the eggs, apple juice and butter. Whisk in the flour, cinnamon and salt until blended. Let the batter rest for about 30 minutes.

Peel and core the apples and slice into ⅓-inch rings. Toss them with the lemon juice to prevent them from discoloring. Pat the slices dry. Preheat the oil in a deep-fryer to 365° F.

Dip the slices, 1 at a time, into the batter and drop carefully into the oil. Cook just a few at a time so that the oil stays close to 365° F. Crowding the pan will result in greasy fritters. Remove them from the oil with a skimmer and drain on paper towels.

Serve warm and pass the sugar.

Remember never to fill your fryer more than half-full with oil.

Jelly Doughnuts

Makes about 1½ dozen

There is not much that beats a freshly made doughnut—successful doughnut companies have made their brand-names into household words. Now you can eat the freshest doughnuts imaginable. If you want to taste one right away, be sure to watch out for the hot jelly.

 1   tablespoon active dry yeast
 ½ cup warm water
 ¼ cup granulated sugar
4½ cups all purpose flour, plus
       more for shaping
 ½ teaspoon ground nutmeg
       (optional)
 ⅔ cup warm milk
 ½ stick butter, melted
 2 large eggs, at room temperature,
       lightly beaten
1½ cups raspberry jelly
 1 beaten egg white
       Vegetable oil, for deep frying
       Cinnamon sugar for coating

In a large bowl, sprinkle yeast over water, add 1 teaspoon of the sugar and let sit for 5 minutes. Stir in 1 cup of the flour and optional nutmeg, cover and let sit at room temperature for 30 minutes, or until bubbly.

With a wooden spoon, stir in milk, butter, eggs and remaining sugar. Sift in remaining flour, beating well after each addition.

Turn the dough onto a floured surface and knead well with floured hands, adding just enough flour so the dough is not sticky.

Place the dough in a large oiled or buttered bowl, turning to coat the dough. Cover the bowl tightly with plastic and set in a warm spot to rise until doubled in size (about 1 hour). Punch down the dough with a floured hand, cover again with oiled plastic and refrigerate until chilled (about 3 hours or overnight).

Turn out the dough onto a lightly floured surface and divide in half. (Cover and refrigerate half of the

Tips:

Remember that yeast is alive and will only raise the dough if you treat it nicely. Use water and milk that is just warm enough to bathe a baby, and let the dough rise in a warm but not hot area.

Fry doughnuts in small batches; over-filling the fryer lowers the heat of the oil and makes for greasy doughnuts.

Time preheating of the oil so it will be ready when the first batch of doughnuts has risen. You can refrigerate some of the risen doughnuts to prevent them from over-rising while you are busy frying and coating the others.

dough.) Roll out the chilled dough to a thickness of ¼ inch. With a floured 3-inch round biscuit cutter, cut the dough into rounds. Spoon a rounded teaspoon of jelly onto the center of half of the rounds and brush the edges with beaten egg white. Top each with a round of plain dough and press to seal the edges.

Line a large tray with waxed paper, and with a large metal spatula transfer the filled doughnuts to the tray. Let rise until doubled in size (30 minutes to 1 hour).

Repeat with the remaining chilled dough. Use the scraps to make more filled doughnuts or simply shape into small balls and fry plain.

In a paper bag, place about 1 cup granulated sugar and set aside. Preheat the oil in a deep-fryer to 365° F. Fry the doughnuts, 3 at a time, carefully turning once to brown on both sides (about 3 minutes). Drain well on paper towels. Toss the warm doughnuts in the cinnamon sugar and enjoy immediately!

Remember never to fill your fryer more than half-full with oil.

Fried Fruit Tarts

Makes 12 tarts

Sometimes these are called "fried pies" or turnovers. There is something special about having a whole fruit tart to yourself, even if it's a small one. These tarts are more transportable than a large tart and a whole lot easier to serve and eat—no plates and forks, just napkins. You can use different fillings for the pastry; apples are a favorite, and so are peaches. Dried fruit that has been soaked and simmered until thick is a traditional filling.

Allow 2 per person. If you have any leftovers, they can be reheated.

The Filling
½ pound dried apricots
1 24-ounce jar unsweetened applesauce
1 cup water
¼ cup sugar

PREPARE THE FILLING

In a medium saucepan, simmer together the apricots, applesauce and water, stirring occasionally, until the apricots are tender and the sauce is thick, about 30 minutes. If desired, add the sugar, depending on the sweetness of the fruit, and set aside to cool completely.

The fruit can be prepared a day ahead and refrigerated for up to 4 days.

PREPARE THE PASTRY

In a large bowl, combine the flour and salt. Add the shortening and cut it into the flour, using a pastry blender or 2 knives, until the mixture resembles coarse meal.

The Pastry
2 pounds prepared pastry dough
  (defrosted if frozen)

OR

1 pound all-purpose flour
1 teaspoon salt
1 cup shortening
⅔ cup ice-cold water

Vegetable oil for deep frying

With a fork, gradually stir enough water into the dough so it can be gathered into a ball.

Divide the home-made (or store-bought) dough into 2 discs, wrap each one in plastic and refrigerate until cold (about 1 hour). The pastry can be made a day ahead.

On a lightly floured surface, roll out half of the dough very thinly. Cut out 6 5-inch circles, using a small saucer as a template. Put about ¼ cup of the fruit onto each round of dough. Moisten the pastry edges with water and fold over half of the dough to enclose the filling in a half-moon shape. Press the edges well to seal. Repeat with the remaining pastry and filling.

Preheat the oil in a deep-fryer to 375° F. Prepare a tray lined with paper towels for draining the tarts.

Fry the tarts 2 to 4 at a time until golden brown (about 3 to 4 minutes). Cool about 30 minutes before serving. They are especially great with vanillia ice cream!

Remember never to fill your fryer more than half-full with oil.

Brown Sugar and Lime Fried Crullers

Makes about 50 crullers

4 eggs, lightly beaten
1 cup brown sugar
2 tablespoon lime zest
⅓ cup melted shortening
⅓ cup whole milk
3½ cups sifted flour
1½ teaspoons cream of tartar
½ teaspoon baking soda
¼ teaspoon salt
½ teaspoon ground cardamom
¼ cup confectioners' sugar for sprinkling
Vegetable shortening for deep frying

In a large mixing bowl, beat eggs and sugar together until well combined. Stir in the lime zest, shortening and milk.

In a separate bowl, whisk together the sifted flour and remaining dry ingredients. Add slowly to the egg mixture, mixing until just combined.

Turn the dough out onto a lightly floured surface and roll into a 12-by-14-inch rectangle. Using a sharp knife, pastry wheel or pizza dough cutter, cut the dough lengthwise into ½-inch strips. Cut the strips in half crosswise. Twist the strips for a decorative look.

Preheat the shortening in a deep-fryer to 365° F.

Fry in batches of 6 until deep golden in color (about 2 minutes per side). Remove to a paper-towel–lined sheet pan to drain. Sprinkle with sugar, and serve warm.

Remember never to fill your fryer more than half-full with oil.

Bayou Bourbon Beignets

6 to 8 servings

While beignets are technically doughnuts, they are more than breakfast food. A warm beignet, covered with so much powdered sugar that it floats into your lap on the first bite, is a lovely treat any time of the day—or night.

Hot, strong, chicory-flavored coffee is the beverage favored to accompany beignets in New Orleans. At the Café du Monde in the French Quarter, you can find crowds of people, nearly 'round the clock, enjoying puffs of snowy white beignets.

4 large eggs, separated
2 cups all-purpose flour
1 teaspoon baking powder
¼ cup sugar
½ teaspoon salt
1¼ cups milk
2 tablespoons bourbon
2 teaspoons lemon zest
  Powdered sugar, for sifting over beignets
  Vegetable oil for deep frying

Beat egg yolks until light in color. In another bowl, sift together flour, baking powder, sugar and salt. Beat in the yolks. Beat in milk, bourbon and lemon zest. Beat egg whites to soft peaks and fold in.

Preheat the oil in a deep-fryer to 360° F.

In small batches, drop batter into oil by large table-spoonfuls, frying until puffed and light golden. Using fryer basket, drain and transfer to paper towels. Sift lots of powdered sugar over the beignets and serve immediately.

Old-Fashioned Cake Doughnuts with Nutmeg

Makes 2 dozen doughnuts and their holes.

1 cup sugar
4 tablespoons unsalted butter, softened
3 large eggs
4½ cups all-purpose flour, plus extra for working dough
4 teaspoons baking powder
1 teaspoon salt
1 teaspoon nutmeg
½ cup milk
  Vegetable oil for deep frying
  Granulated sugar or confectioners' sugar for coating

In an electric mixer, cream together sugar and butter until very light in color. Beat in the eggs, 1 at a time, until the mixture is very fluffy and light.

Sift together the flour, baking powder, salt and nutmeg. On low speed, blend the dry ingredients into the butter mixture. Do not overmix. Gradually blend in the milk. If mixture does not seem moist and malleable, blend in an additional tablespoon of milk.

Preheat the oil in a deep-fryer to 365° F. Cover a sheet pan or large plate with brown paper or paper towels.

Put either granulated sugar or confectioners' sugar into a clean, brown paper bag.

On a lightly floured surface, use your fingertips to pat the dough out to a ⅓-inch thickness. Dip a 3-inch doughnut cutter in flour and cut out doughnuts and holes. Gather the scraps, pat them out and cut more doughnuts. Toss out the scraps after the second cut.

Carefully add the doughnuts to the hot oil; fry them in small batches, turning them with long tongs to

brown both sides (about 1½ minutes per side). Using a fryer basket, drain and transfer to paper-lined sheet pan.

Cool completely before tossing doughnuts in the bag with sugar. Serve promptly.

Remember never to fill your fryer more than half-full with oil.

Honey-Soaked Fried Dough Loops

Makes 20 4-inch pastries

These delicious tidbits are at their absolute best when served with hot, strong coffee!

The Dough
4 large eggs
2 teaspoons vegetable oil
2 cups all-purpose flour
½ teaspoon baking soda
Pinch of salt

Vegetable oil for deep frying
Cornstarch for sprinkling
rolling surface

PREPARE THE DOUGH

In a medium bowl, whisk the eggs lightly. Stir in the oil, flour, baking soda and salt. If the dough is sticky, stir in an additional ¼ cup flour. Knead until smooth and elastic.

Preheat the oil in a deep fryer to 365° F.

Cut the dough in half; wrap half in plastic wrap and set it aside. Cover a surface liberally with cornstarch.

On the cornstarch, roll one dough half into a thick tube and cut it into 5 pieces. Work with the pieces one at a time and cover the remainder with a clean dishtowel. Using a rolling pin and plenty of cornstarch to prevent sticking, roll the dough into a very thin, 2-by-12-inch sheet. Cut the sheet lengthwise into 2 pieces.

One at a time, wrap a strip of dough around the four fingers of your hand in very loose loops. Seal the ends together by moistening them with a little water and pressing them together.

The Syrup
  1 cup sugar
  1 cup water
  1 tablespoon lemon juice
  2 tablespoons honey

Slip the center of the looped dough over the handle of a wooden spoon and gently slide it into the hot oil. As the dough is frying, swirl the spoon handle in the center of the loops to bring out the shapes. Fry until golden (about 2 minutes). Turn and fry the second side. Using fryer basket, drain and transfer to paper towels.

Shape and fry the remaining dough in the same manner. Repeat procedure with the half of the dough that was set aside.

PREPARE THE SYRUP

In a medium saucepan, stir together the sugar, the water, lemon juice and honey. Bring to a boil over medium heat and cook until thickened (about 10 minutes).

Dip the pastries into the syrup one at a time and drain on a cooling rack until dry.

Remember never to fill your fryer more than half-full with oil.

Mexi-Churros

4 to 6 servings

Churros, originally from Spain but made famous by Mexico, are simply deep–fried strips of batter that are dusted with powdered sugar and enjoyed as sweet treats.

1¼ cups water
2 tablespoons butter
1½ cups flour
Pinch of salt
2 eggs
Vegetable oil for deep frying
Confectioners' sugar for dusting

In a large saucepan, bring the water and butter to a boil. Add the flour and salt and beat with a wooden spoon until smooth. Remove the pan from the stove and beat for 1 minute. Add the eggs one at a time, beating well until smooth. Transfer the mixture to a gallon-size sealable plastic bag.

Prepare a tray lined with crumpled paper towels for draining the churros.

Preheat the oil in a deep-fryer to 365° F.

With a scissors, snip 1 inch from the corner of the plastic bag and squeeze a few lengths of dough into the hot oil. Fry until golden. Drain the churros on the paper towels. Repeat with the remaining churro dough. The churros should be dusted with sugar when hot and can be eaten hot or cold.

Remember never to fill your fryer more than half-full with oil.

Apple Doughnuts

Makes about 20

4 cups all-purpose flour
½ cup sugar
1½ teaspoons baking powder
1 teaspoon ground allspice or cinnamon
  Pinch of salt
2 eggs
½ cup apple juice
1 cup applesauce
¼ cup vegetable oil
  Vegetable oil for deep frying
  Confectioners' sugar with cinnamon

In a large bowl, combine the flour, sugar, baking powder, allspice (or cinnamon) and salt.

In a separate bowl, mix together the eggs, apple juice, applesauce and oil. Pour the liquid mixture into the flour mixture and stir into a dough.

Preheat the oil in a deep-fryer to 375° F.

With floured hands, tear the dough into small evenly-sized pieces. Add 4 of the pieces at a time to the oil and cook, turning them if needed, until golden brown, 3 to 4 minutes. Adding too many doughnuts to the oil at one time will lower the oil temperature, increase the cooking time and make the doughnuts greasy. Drain the doughnuts on paper towels and repeat with the remaining dough. Serve fresh.

For a sweeter twist, mix a teaspoon of cinnamon with a cup of confectioners' sugar in a bag, add the warm doughnuts a few at a time and toss. Or, mix sugar and cinnamon together in a sugar shaker and let your kids powder their own doughnuts.

Remember never to fill your fryer more than half-full with oil.

Deep-Fried Bananas with Ice Cream

4 servings

These battered bananas are a popular Indonesian street snack and dessert. To "gild the lily," drizzle the bananas and ice cream with dark rum or dust with ground cinnamon.

½ cup all-purpose white flour
¼ cup confectioners' sugar
½ teaspoon baking powder
¼ teaspoon salt
1 large egg
½ cup water
4 slightly under-ripe bananas, peeled and cut in half, crosswise
Vegetable oil for deep frying

4 scoops vanilla ice cream

In a shallow bowl, whisk together flour, sugar, baking powder and salt until well-mixed.

In another small bowl, whisk egg until frothy; whisk in the water. Gradually whisk the wet mixture into the dry ingredients to make a smooth, thin batter.

Preheat the oil in a deep-fryer to 350° F. Four halves at a time, dip bananas in the batter and add to the oil. Fry until golden (about 3 minutes). Drain briefly on paper towels. Repeat with the remaining bananas.

Serve two halves per person, topped with vanilla ice cream.

Remember never to fill your fryer more than half-full with oil.

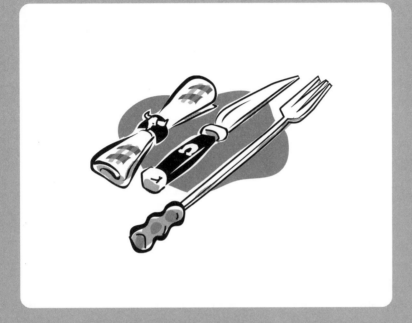

Helpful Hints

Deep Frying Dos and Don'ts

Deep-frying is a wonderful way to cook food; the hot oil quickly sears the outside, locking in flavor and adding that delectable crunch. Foods cook quickly because they are completely surrounded by intense heat. When food is immersed in hot oil, the moisture near the surface of the food turns into steam. As the steam slows down, the surface gets hotter and begins to brown. When all the moisture has cooked away, the food begins to absorb fat, so you want to remove it from the hot oil just before this point. With the proper technique, fried foods absorb much less oil than you might expect.

The correct oil temperature can be anywhere from 325° to 400° F., depending on what's being cooked. Small pieces of food should be cooked at the higher end of the temperature range and for a shorter length of time; make sure all the pieces are of uniform size so that they cook at the same rate.

Larger items require a lower oil temperature so that the outside doesn't burn before the inside is cooked. Dense foods should be fried more slowly than porous ones. Sometimes a recipe will direct you to "blanch" the food in water or oil, which means to pre-cook it at a lower temperature, let it cool, then finish it at a higher temperature; this is a favorite technique for crispy French fries.

Have everything in place before you begin frying; set up a small table near the cooker to place food and tools on, and have ready a baking sheet lined with paper towels or brown paper bags to receive and drain the cooked food.

You'll want to use plenty of oil, but never fill the pot more than halfway, as the oil may bubble up significantly when you add the food. A tall narrow pot makes that less dangerous. Some turkey-frying pots, such as the New Braunfels Smoker

Company's 26-quart cooker, come with handy oil-level indicator lines for specific weights of turkeys. If your pot doesn't have lines, an easy way to determine how much oil you need is to put the turkey in the pot, add enough water to cover, then measure the water after removing the turkey. Be sure to dry the turkey well, both inside and out, before you fry it!

A generous amount of oil allows the food to move freely for even cooking and ensures that the temperature of the oil doesn't drop drastically when food is added. Add food a little at a time to minimize the temperature drop, cooking it in several batches if necessary. Having the food at room temperature and wiping any moisture from the surface will also help to maintain the temperature of the oil. And never add fresh oil to the pot in the middle of frying—the unheated oil would lower the temperature too significantly.

A good frying thermometer is essential for determining when the oil is ready; while some cooks maintain that you can tell how hot the oil is by how quickly it browns a piece of bread, this is unreliable because the moisture content of bread varies. If your pot is tall, you'll want a nice, long thermometer that will reach the oil easily. Use the thermometer to check the oil temperature as the food cooks so that you can adjust the heat to keep the oil at a consistent heat.

Foods are often coated before frying for a crisper exterior. The coating can be a simple seasoned flour mixture or cornmeal, breadcrumbs, a thin batter-like tempura or a thicker fritter-type batter. Drying the surface of the food or dusting it with flour will help the batter to stick—rather than slip off—during cooking. Fine breadcrumbs will absorb less fat during frying, but coarser crumbs will give you a crisper crust. Sugar added to batter will speed the browning as the sugar caramelizes.

Once the food is cooked, remove it with tongs, a wire mesh skimmer, a slotted spoon, a strainer basket or the insert that came with your pot; let the food drain briefly over the pot, then transfer it to layered paper towels or brown paper bags for draining. You can hold fried foods in a low oven (about 225° F.) for a while if you are cooking a second batch. Salt can draw out moisture from food and make it soggy, so salt just before serving.

Boilin' Tips

While a vigorous boil is important for pastas and firm vegetables like corn, dishes like soups and stews require only a gentle simmer. A rapid boil will toughen meat fibers and make vegetables fall apart. It's a good idea to brown meats for stewing in a skillet first, which will deepen the flavor of the finished dish.

Be sure to use a perforated insert when you boil foods like corn or lobster so that you can lift them from the water easily.

Safety First

- Propane cookers are meant to be used outdoors only. Set the cooker on a non-combustible flat surface, such as concrete, brick or earth.
- Before using a gas cooker, check all the connections, hoses and valves with a mixture of 1 part liquid detergent to 3 parts water; brush it on generously and turn on the gas; if you see any bubbling, turn off the gas, tighten the connections and check them again.
- Keep children and pets away from a boiling or frying pot. Move slowly and carefully, yourself, when moving around the pot.
- Use a pot with short side handles, not a long handle, which can be easily caught or knocked.
- Always keep handy a set of mitts that are long enough to cover your forearms. Wear long pants and a long-sleeve shirt as well.
- For deep-frying, use a pot that is larger in diameter than the heat source beneath it, so any drips over the edge are less apt to flame up.
- Never fill the pot more than half-full with oil.

- Never cover the pot while heating oil.
- Never try to move a flaming pot of oil.
- Have on hand a fire extinguisher formulated for oil fires. Also have the lid handy to quickly place over the pot and deprive any flames of oxygen.
- Never use water to try and extinguish an oil fire, as it will only float the oil and spread the flames.
- Never leave hot or cooling liquids or oil unattended. Constantly monitor the oil temperature with a thermometer.
- Dry foods well before adding them to hot oil, and add them slowly to minimize bubbling up; use long tongs, or use a perforated fry basket for small items like fries.
- A large item like a turkey will cause the hot oil to bubble up quite dramatically, so dip it partially in the oil then pull it back up a few times to vaporize the excess moisture. The New Braunfels Smoker Company's 26-quart cooker comes with a T-Star lifter and handle that makes immersion and removal of large items much easier.
- Disconnect the cooker from the propane tank before storing it in a garage. Store the tank separately outside.

All About Oil

In the "good old days" the substance of choice for deep-fat frying was usually a rendered animal fat such as lard, which comes from pork. Lard gives fried foods a wonderful flavor but is unfortunately high in saturated fat. Palm oil, coconut oil and even solid vegetable shortening can also be used for deep-frying, but these are also high in saturated fat.

Today's healthier choices for deep-frying are oils made from grains, vegetables or fruit, such as corn, safflower, canola, soybean, peanut or olive oil (refined, not virgin or extra-virgin). Remember that although all oils have about the same calorie content—"light" is a term that refers only to flavor—today's oils *are* significantly lower in saturated fats and contain no cholesterol.

Another advantage of these oils is their higher "smoke point," which makes them better for deep frying. When an oil reaches its smoke point, it begins to change chemically, giving off smelly fumes and developing unpleasant flavors.

Grain, vegetable and fruit oils all have a smoke point of over 400° F., but you should never heat oil to over 400° F., because excessive heat makes the oil deteriorate faster. Always use a thermometer to gauge the temperature, and never leave hot oil unattended. Fresh oil will not actually burst into flame until it reaches about 700° F., but that stage can potentially be reached at progressively lower temperatures each time that the oil is used.

The chart below shows the range of smoke points for a variety of deep-frying oils:

Safflower	450° F.
Grapeseed	446° F.
Canola (rapeseed)	437° F.
Soybean	410° F.
Corn	410° F.
Peanut	410° F.
Sesame (light)	410° F.
Olive (refined, not extra-virgin or virgin)	410° F.
Solid shortening	370° F.

PAIRING FOODS WITH OILS:

Any of the oils listed at left are fine for deep-frying. What is labeled "vegetable oil" at the supermarket is most often pure soybean oil or a blend of canola and soybean. You will also find blends of canola and corn oil. Some oils have a definite flavor; peanut, light sesame and corn oils have a "nutty" taste, while soy and canola oils have a mild "bean" flavor. Peanut oil is traditional for many Asian dishes and a favorite with deep-fried turkey aficionados. For delicate or sweet fried foods, such as tempura or fried sweets, safflower oil is a good choice because it is nearly flavorless. Grapeseed oil is also delicate but expensive and hard to find. For Italian fried specialties, olive oil is an obvious choice.

STORING AND USING OILS:

Since deep frying requires a fair amount of oil, it's important to protect your investment. Light, heat and oxygen all cause oil to deteriorate; store fresh oil in a cool, dark place. If you live in a warm climate, keep the oil in the refrigerator, particularly safflower oil, which becomes rancid more easily than other oils. Let any refrigerated oil come to room temperature before heating, to avoid splattering.

The longer oil sits over heat, the more it deteriorates; don't preheat frying oil any longer than necessary, and turn off the heat underneath as soon as you have removed the last batch of food.

Liquid and salt also cause oils to break down; dry food well before adding it to hot oil, and salt foods after they are fried rather than before.

Beyond Your Backyard

With high-tech speed, our cooking horizons have expanded to include the most obscure regions and ingredients. You can surf the Internet and discover a plethora of recipes, from traditional Korean oil-crisped seaweed to newfangled Scottish deep-fried Mars Bars!

The frying/boiling pot is a great place to explore this global buffet, and there is a world of flavorings available to help you do that. Dry spice rubs are a great way to flavor meat, poultry or fish before deep-frying. For poultry, rub the mixture both under and over the skin. Oklahoma Joe's™ has some terrific Kansas City–style rubs, including Original BBQ seasoning, Steak seasoning, Hog Rub & Yard Bird seasoning and Sweet & Spicy seasoning. You can order them online at www.oklahomajoesbbq.com. Or use your favorite Mexican chili powder, Indian curry blend or Asian five-spice powder. Sweet and spicy "jerk" seasoning from Jamaica is another great rub, and you can make it yourself or use a prepared version.

Marinades also bring vibrant flavors to deep-fried meat, poultry or fish, and the options are endless. You can choose the traditional steeping method or use an injector to direct the marinade deep into the food. Try New Braunfels Smoker Company's Texas Style Zesty Marinade or Creole Butter Marinade. (To order marinade or injector, call 1-800-232-3398.)

Another alternative is to deep-fry or boil foods more plainly and spoon on the flavor at the end with a zesty sauce. For a down-home flavor, try Oklahoma Joe's™ BBQ sauce with chicken, beef or pork. But explore the possibilities from the international pantry as well. Most of these sauces can be quickly made at home, or you can find them already prepared at the supermarket or smaller ethnic markets. Instead of predictable butter for boiled corn or lobsters, for instance, serve a basil or artichoke pesto; to accent a mild pot roast, boiled fish or simple steamed mussels, try tart Tuscan salsa verde made with parsley, capers and garlic. Make familiar French fries brand new again by serving them European-style with garlicky aioli sauce instead of ketchup. Top fried chicken or fish with fresh mint chutney from India or spicy Moroccan charmoula. And don't forget fresh and easy Mexican salsas of tomatoes or fruits for topping deep-fried steaks, poultry or fish.

Now that you've got the know-how and so many easy and delicious possibilities at your fingertips, it's time to fire up that cooker!

Equipment and Accessories

Most sporting-goods stores, mass merchants and many hardware stores sell propane gas cookers for outdoor deep frying, boiling and steaming. Look for a sturdy heavy-gauge steel stand with welded joints that will hold the filled pot without any danger of tipping. The gas burner should have at least 160,000 BTUs with a fully adjustable regulator for heat control.

HERE ARE ADDITIONAL ACCESSORIES YOU WILL NEED:

- **Tank of Propane Gas:** The tank is not sold with the cooker, so you will need to purchase it separately from a propane gas company or hardware store and return there to have it refilled. Bring the hose from the cooker along with you to make sure the fitting is compatible with the tank.
- **Pots:** For deep-frying a turkey, you want a tall, narrow aluminum or stainless steel pot that holds at least 26 quarts (6.5 gallons), which will cook the turkey more efficiently than a shorter, wider stockpot. The pot should come with a lid and a perforated strainer-basket insert. You can cook up to an 18-pound turkey in this size pot, and it's also great for seafood boils, steaming and big batches of soups, chili and stews. For smaller amounts, you will also want a 2-gallon pot.
- **Oven Mitts:** Choose grill-type heat-resistant mitts that will cover and protect your forearms. Get two sets so a helper will be ready to assist you with trickier jobs like lowering a turkey into hot oil.
- **Deep-Fry Thermometer:** Buy a stainless steel thermometer that will stand up to the heat without melting. It should have a clip to attach it to the side of the pot, should be long enough to reach the fat in a deep pot easily and should register up to 500° F.

- **Instant-Read Thermometer:** When deep-frying meats, this item is essential for determining when the proper interior temperature of food has been reached.
- **Perforated skimmer or ladle:** To remove smaller items from simmering water or hot oil, you will need a perforated metal skimmer rather than a slotted spoon, which, although appropriate for some deep-frying jobs, is often too small and retains too much oil. An Asian brass wire-mesh skimmer also works well, and the wooden handle does not conduct heat.
- **Tongs:** To slip larger items into hot oil, and then remove them once cooked, a long pair of spring-loaded metal tongs is very useful.
- **Marinade Injector:** This syringe allows you to inject marinades deep into poultry, meat or fish for an especially flavorful and moist result.

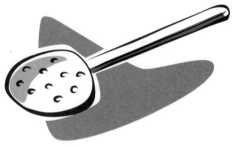

Index

Index

D

E

F

G

Notes